BRITISH INDIA
Post-War
Passenger Ships

William H. Miller

AMBERLEY

For Richard De Kerbrech,
David Hutchings and David Williams.

Three splendid men – historians, authors and first-class ocean liner enthusiasts.

First published 2014

Amberley Publishing
The Hill, Stroud
Gloucestershire, GL5 4EP

www.amberley-books.com

Copyright © William H. Miller, 2014

The right of William H. Miller to be identified as the Author of this work has been asserted in accordance with the Copyrights, Designs and Patents Act 1988.

ISBN 978 1 4456 3591 0 (print)
ISBN 978 1 4456 3607 8 (ebook)

British Library Cataloguing in Publication Data.
A catalogue record for this book is available from the British Library.

Typeset in 11pt on 12pt Sabon LT Std.
Typesetting by Amberley Publishing.
Printed in the UK.

ACKNOWLEDGMENTS

Like the running of a British passenger ship, it takes many hands to assemble such a book. To a great extent, I operate as an organizer, designer, and collector of facts, anecdotes and recollections. First and foremost, my great thanks to Amberley Publishing for taking on this title and, in doing so, hopefully adding something to our understanding of bygone passenger ships and their operations. Special thanks to Robert Lloyd for his brilliant cover material. Highest thanks also to Richard Turnwald for his superb photo contributions. This book is also possible due to the splendid research of authors Duncan Haws and Peter Kohler, both producing excellent fleet histories of British India. Thank you as well to Martin Carvalho for his generous foreword.

Further, very insightful contributions have come from former BI staff and passengers including David Andrews, Hans Andresen, Harry Atkinson, Robert Bell, Keith Byass, Captain Bob Ellingham, Neville Gordon, Brian Gregory, John Smith and Alan Wells. Special thanks also to Howard Franklin, Michael Hadgis and Anthony La Forgia.

British India advertising posters.

CONTENTS

FOREWORD

Even as a youngster growing up in Goa I had heard of BI – the great British India Company. So many families and friends were connected to that company, mostly by serving aboard as crew members. There was, in the 1950s, a sort of prestige, a local importance, of serving aboard a British vessel and especially a luxury passenger ship. BI – as well as P&O – had the highest prestige.

As a very young man, I traveled from Bombay to Durban in the *Karanja* and later returned on board the *Kampala*. It was then the travel experience of a lifetime – casting off from Bombay, seeing the vastness of the Indian Ocean, stopping in the Seychelles, reaching far-off East Africa and, of course, the sheer experience of shipboard life. I recall the teak decks, the sound of the ship's whistle, the food in the dining room, being served, the British officers in their immaculately white uniforms. I also remember the cabin with four bunks, a sink, rattan chair and an open porthole allowing in the sounds of the sea. There were idyllic, sun-filled days and nights highlighted by what seemed to be a few thousand stars overhead. Out on deck, those ships had their own sounds – the whipping of the wind, the rattling of cables and pulleys, the uninterrupted throb of the engines far below.

For me, being aboard those BI ships was a very great experience. It was a kind of magical notation of earlier days. I might as well have been aboard the *Queen Mary*. I thank my friend Bill Miller, who – with this book – reminded me of a special travel experience that was, difficult to believe, now some fifty years ago.

Martin Carvalho
New Jersey, USA
Spring 2014

INTRODUCTION

The name itself, the British India Steam Navigation Company Limited, stirs up images of the imperial past, that long-ago British imperial past, and of course of a distant time – and an evocative and, in some ways, romantic era. Commonly known as 'the BI', this London-based firm was owned in fact by an even larger and mightier British ship owner, P&O, the Peninsular & Oriental Steam Navigation Company. However, British India maintained a separate fleet, one that was for many decades very important, in fact vital, to the British Empire and its last remnants.

BI's passenger ships in particular were important for the steady, uninterrupted flow of representatives of the Crown: the colonial governors and high commissioners, doctors and teachers, the police and troops, their families, traders and, of course, tourists. Then there were the more localized passenger trades transporting, usually in deck class, the Indians, the Chinese, Malaysians, South and East Africans and, even more remote, the Seychellois. They were also important for the exchange of cargos (British manufactured goods going outward in exchange for local items such as cotton, textiles, spices, nuts and especially prized minerals).

The handsome looking sisters *Kenya* and *Uganda* were perhaps British India's best-known post-Second World War passenger ships. They were classic combination passenger-cargo ships, then quite commonly used in colonial service. In themselves, they symbolized an era. They provided steadfast links to and from the mother country. They were important links in the great imperial chain. But as the Union Jacks came down in far-off African lands, so their steady employment ended as well.

The *Kenya* left East African waters in June 1969, running the last British-flag passenger service to what had been colonial East Africa. By the late sixties, however, with decolonization well underway, the passenger as well as the freight trades aboard British flag ships had withered substantially; the colonial trade all but disintegrated, remaining travelers defected to the airlines and even the cargoes moved to newly formed, nationalized African shipping companies. Struggling with aging ships, high operating costs and, in particular, the demanding seamen's unions, the once bright sun for British passenger shipping, once the largest, most extensive network on earth, was indeed setting.

When the *Uganda* finished her career in 1986 in the silent abandonment of some Far Eastern scrap yard, it concluded the story of this fine ship and was just about the final chapter of not just the East African liner service, but British India's passenger ships altogether. The *Uganda* was in fact the last ship to have the once very recognizable BI funnel colors of all black with white stripes. Historically, the BI name was officially dissolved much earlier, in 1971, when it was fully integrated into parent P&O's passenger and freight divisions. The very last link came two years after the *Uganda* was sold for scrapping, in 1988, when the *Nancowry*, the former *Karanja* and last remaining BI passenger ship, went to the scrappers.

Living on the doorstep of New York City in the 1950s and 1960s, I knew of British India only from a great distance. I knew them from the brochures set out in the Cunard offices on Lower Broadway and from Laurence Dunn's wonderful enlightening books. Even more so than the liners of, say, Union-Castle and P&O, BI ships such as the *Karanja*, *Amra*, *Sangola* and *Dumra* seemed very exotic, very faraway. Now, some fifty or so years later, I am very happy to write this review, far too short in ways, but then meant to be a grand reminder of one of Britain's greatest and most interesting ship owners. It is of their final passenger ship fleet. My only regret is that when I was offered a lecture spot on board the school ship *Uganda* back in 1980 I had to decline. That would have been my only direct experience with the British India Steam Navigation Company Limited.

Bill Miller
Secaucus, New Jersey
Spring 2014

BRITISH INDIA: A BRIEF HISTORY

Without question, the British India Steam Navigation Company Limited was one of the greatest of all British ship owners. The company dated back to 1862 when it was incorporated by a Scottish merchant, William Mackinnon. As its name readily suggests, its basic trade was with the subcontinent of India. Growth was rapid and within a decade, by 1872, trading was expanded to Malaya, Singapore and, most significantly for that time, a mail contract was obtained between Aden and Zanzibar. In the long reign of Queen Victoria it was also the age of great British imperialism – the British Empire – and BI, as it was called, played a significant part connecting those far-off, outlying colonies. Further corporate strength was derived from the delivery of the all-important mails, delivered by P&O steamers to Aden and then transferred to waiting BI steamers bound for East African ports.

Expansion continued and in 1887 Mackinnon founded the Imperial British East Africa Company and then, soon thereafter, he planned to set up a railway route from Mombasa to the distant interior of Uganda. Soon BI steamers themselves were trading between London, Suez and East Africa. By 1895, as construction of the railway began, BI steamers were delivering the likes of engineering personnel as well as structural materials from Britain and then also great numbers of laborers from India across to Mombasa. That route was later extended to other ports along the East African coast, including Mozambique, and all as BI itself grew and greatly prospered. Elsewhere, business flourished as well. By the turn of the century, for example, British India steamers were carrying as much as 90 per cent of the export of Burmese rice. This in turn induced a service up to Japan.

Just months before the start of the First World War, in May 1914, British India amalgamated with P&O, its long-time trading cohort in eastern services. P&O, being the larger company, dominated this arrangement, with twelve directors from P&O and eight from British India. In the 1930s, during the Great Depression, BI was all but unaffected since the likes of the Indian and East African services were reliant on government contracts, delivering mail and supplies, and a virtually continuous flow of government-related passengers in upper-deck first and second class and still far greater numbers in lower-deck third and deck classes.

Up until the start of the Second World War, in the summer of 1939, British India flourished in services to East Africa and across the Indian Ocean and even out to the Far East.

During the Second World War, however, BI lost no less than fifty-one ships – or over 320,000 tons of shipping – and then resumed operations in 1945–46 with revised priorities. With India soon to go independent (in 1947), the African trades were seen as more reliable, more long-lasting. But while British India quickly replaced lost tonnage, including a new generation of passenger ships, further change was indeed on the horizon. The 1950s were still prosperous, busy, profitable, very much 'the good old days'. By the 1960s, however, it was all changing – the great imperial sunset as it was often termed. As author Duncan Haws wrote, 'The end of the Second World War created a different world. Imperialism was all but outmoded and independence became the aim of nationalist forces. America in particular, officially the most powerful nation on earth, backed this new era and saw commercial advantages for its own, immense industry. The effect on British shipping was that of a gradual cutback in her merchant as well as naval fleets as new nations built up their own shipping interests. British India was one of the greatest victims of these changes.'

Fleet changes were inevitable. The company branched out, going into tankers in the mid-1950s (but with actual deliveries of ships beginning in 1959) and then, in 1958 and after a century-long association, bought out Mackinnon, Mackenzie & Company and finally terminated its role as managing agents. Another change soon to come was the elimination by the British government of trooping by sea. By 1960 the company was still quite strong with sixty-three ships (but comparatively 100 less than in 1920).

Decolonization was in full swing by the 1960s and near constant changes, declines and withdrawals occurred within the once vast BI fleet. In an era attempting to reduce losses and increase efficiency, P&O took full control by 1971 and reorganized BI into its separate passenger, cargo and bulk shipping divisions. Integration was steady and by the mid-1970s only the few remaining passenger ships retained their traditional BI funnel colors of black with two white bands.

British India 'line service', using the aged *Dwarka*, finished altogether in 1982. The *Uganda* was the last direct link to the great and illustrious British India Steam Navigation Company Limited and she was sold off to Taiwanese scrappers four years later.

1

MODURA, MODASA, MANTOLA, MATIANA AND *MULBERA* (1921–25)

'They were very much workaday ships that gave long, in ways almost exceptional service', noted Captain Ian Tompkins. 'They helped revive BI passenger services, especially the "Home Line" between the UK and East Africa, after the Second World War'. As peace in Europe came in May 1945 and then in the Pacific that August, BI was planning for the prompt resumption of its passenger and freight services, restoring surviving ships and building new tonnage, especially for its vast passenger operations. While India would become independent in 1947, it would still rely for years to come on the highly useful and skilled operations of BI. Great potential remained. The greatest area of interest had shifted, however, and was now in British East Africa, which was rich in much-needed minerals. Post-war South and East Africa both had enormous importance as well as an expansive future according to both BI management and the government's colonial office. There was rising emigration to South Africa, vast mineral wealth of the two Rhodesians and, possibly most promising of all, the great potential of the groundnut scheme in Tanganyika. The latter was intended to provide Britain with badly needed vegetable oil and fodder as well as to encourage a huge wave of British settlers away from the war weary, heavily rationed and bankrupted mother country. The plan was to develop, in the late 1940s and early 1950s, 3 million acres of farmland. Nearly £30 million of otherwise much-needed government funds was poured into the soon to be much publicized project.

Alone, the Groundnut Scheme sparked great appeal. Increasing numbers corresponded to the promise of great trading conditions. European emigration to East Africa doubled in the early 1950s, while the flow of Indians to East Africa tripled since just before the war in 1939.

British India was indeed encouraged. In addition to restoring pre-war tonnage, the company would invest £13 million, much of it gained from wartime insurance monies, for almost twenty new ships. Among these were no less than eleven passenger ships: two larger ships for the India–East Africa run, two small East African coastal ships, three 'S' ships for the India–Far East run and four 'D' ships for the Bombay–Persian Gulf run.

Unfortunately, the Groundnut Scheme was a huge failure. In fact, the East African Groundnut Scheme was post-war Britain's equivalent of the Millennium Dome. In pursuit of an ambitious, high-spirited objective, millions of pounds of taxpayers' money was poured diligently into what was called 'a sump of official incompetence'. Begun soon after the war ended in 1947 by the Labour government, the scheme's aim was to grow peanuts in Tanganyika (now Tanzania) as a contribution to both the African and the British economies and to alleviate a world shortage of fats. Unfortunately, the scheme was ill planned, failed to allow for the area's soil and rainfall, and employed unsuitable agricultural methods, including the wrong kind of machinery for the terrain. Nor had local traditions and attitudes been taken into account. The scheme's most successful crop, it was later written, was a bountiful harvest of official 'gobbledegook'.

The plan called for the clearing of 5 million acres of land in the first five years and the creation of a new deep-water port, Mtwara, and railway in Tanganyika, and was expected to create 32,000 jobs for African workers. The project was suggested originally by the United Africa Company, a subsidiary of Unilever, but was soon handed over to the government's Overseas Food Corporation.

Within two years, by 1949, it was clear that things were going badly wrong. In the House of Commons, in July 1950, the British minister of food, admitted that the scheme had been pushed forward at breakneck speed and the methods used had not been adequately tested.

End of the line: the *Mulbera* waiting at the London Docks after her long career. (British India)

Classic lines: the *Mulbera* at sea. (British India)

Outward bound: another ship of the sturdy M Class, the *Modasa*, loading at Marseilles on an outward voyage to East African ports. (Marius Bar)

The Overseas Food Corporation appointed a working party, which reported at the end of September that the scheme was costing six times as much to produce the crops as the crops were worth. The writing was on the wall and the effective abandonment of the Groundnut Scheme was announced in January 1951. The debts were written off to the tune of £36.5 million. In the end, no one seemed eager to acknowledge responsibility.

While there were other surviving passenger ships from pre-war days, we shall concentrate and begin with the five surviving so-called M3 Class ships – *Madura, Modasa, Mantola, Matiana* and *Mulbera*. BI was indeed fortunate to have them to resume home line services. Not modern or especially luxurious and certainly not speedy, they were nevertheless vital in restoring BI's services out of the UK and especially to and from East Africa. They were used, beginning in March 1946, on sailings mostly from London to ports along the East African coast, but also on occasion to India or temporarily on other BI routes.

Built between 1921 and 1925, and with a sixth sister, the *Malda*, being sunk in 1942, they could carry in their post-war years approximately 175 one-class passengers each. Few cabins had private bathroom facilities while public areas consisted of a smoking room, music room and dining room, which could accommodate just about all passengers at one sitting.

These veterans – known in the fleet as 'the Old Reliables' – were gradually retired in the early 1950s. Fetching about £100,000 each in scrap, the *Mantiana* was the first to go, being delivered to scrappers in March 1952 and was soon joined by the *Mantola* and *Madura*. Two years later and with scrap metal prices falling to £60,000 each, the *Modasa* went for breaking in January 1954 and finally the *Mulbera*, the last of these old ships, finished her days at Inverkeithing that April.

2

EMPIRE TROOPER (1922)

British India had its own troopships – ships such as the subsequent *Dilwara* and *Dunera* – but also managed a post-war troopship on behalf of the Ministry of Transport. She was the *Empire Trooper*, built in 1922 by the Vulcan Werke shipyard of Hamburg for the Hamburg–South America Line as their *Cap Norte*. She and a sister, the *Antonio Delfino*, were sensible, very sturdy single-stackers used in the Hamburg–east coast of South America service, sailing to Rio de Janeiro, Santos, Montevideo and Buenos Aires. They were three-class ships, with berthing for 184 in first class, 334 in third class and 1,368 in steerage. Twin screw ships, they were powered by steam triple expansion engines and could make up to 13½ knots.

The 13,615-grt ship was chartered to North German Lloyd for two years, beginning in 1932, and sailed as their *Sierra Salvada* before reverting to the Hamburg–South America service and her original name. She was in Pernambuco in Brazil when the Second World War began and eventually made an attempt to return to Germany, but was intercepted on 9 October and promptly captured by the British in waters north of Iceland. First used as a block ship at Scapa Flow, she was refitted as a troopship in 1940 and renamed *Empire Trooper*. Thereafter she was managed by British India. Damaged in gunfire with the Nazi heavy cruiser *Admiral Hipper* on Christmas Day 1940, she was repaired, survived the war and continued in post-war trooping duties.

Refitted at Falmouth in 1949, she was outfitted as a peacetime trooper, carrying 336 cabin passengers and 924 troops on voyages mostly for the Ministry of Defence. Her tonnage was hereafter listed as 14,106.

In April 1955 the thirty-three-year-old ship was retired and promptly sold to the British Iron & Steel Company for demolition at Inverkeithing in Scotland. Departing under tow from Southampton on 9 April, she was handed over to the breakers on the 14th. But while awaiting her turn for demolition, the anchored ship caught fire in May and then sank. She was raised on 19 June and afterward the breaking-up commenced.

Dressed in flags: the white-hulled *Empire Trooper* was the former German passenger ship *Cap Norte*. (P&O)

3

RAJULA (1926)

'In her later, final years, we sometimes had trouble just keeping her going. We couldn't find replacement parts and actually had to make them ourselves, at the BI marine workshop in Calcutta', remembered Captain Ian Tompkins.

She and her sister *Rohna* (sunk during the Second World War, in July 1943) were largely unnoticed, but had one distinction in the annals of passenger shipping. When completed in 1926 they had the greatest passenger capacities of any deep-sea passenger liners anywhere. As built, the 8,478-grt *Rajula* was certified for 37 first class and 135 second class, but an extraordinary 4,300 deck class. This gave the ship a full capacity of 4,472 passengers. Two years later, in 1928, the 479-foot-long *Rajula* established a record of her very own – an extraordinary 5,113 deck class passengers were onboard for a voyage from Singapore to Madras. They were mostly Hajj pilgrims on their way to Jeddah and Mecca.

Built by British India's preferred Barclay, Curle & Company at Glasgow and launched on 22 September 1926, the ship cost almost £233,000 to build. She entered service in November, and then sailed on a delivery voyage out to India. She and her sister served purposely on the Madras–Penang–Singapore route.

The steam triple expansion, 15-knot, twin screw *Rajula* was called to war duties in the fall of 1939 and was soon used for carrying Indian troops from Bombay to Port Suez. In 1941 she was rerouted to more Eastern waters, carrying Indian forces to Singapore and then returned with evacuees until the city fell to the Japanese on 15 February 1942. She soon began to move about, carrying Australian troops from Colombo, then (in July 1943) was in the Mediterranean to take part in the Sicily landings and then back to the East for service as an ambulance transport. She sailed to and from Rangoon, carrying troops outward from India and returning with patients. The troop decks on ships such as the *Rajula* could only be used for men while the wards were closed off, mainly to avoid infection and for hygiene. By the war's end, in the summer of 1945, the *Rajula* was regularly trooping between Calcutta and Malaysia.

Resuming regular British India sailings in 1946, the *Rajula* had a post-war refit and reappeared with a modified, much

Early days: the classic *Rajula* as built. (British India)

reduced passenger capacity – 37 first class, 133 second class and, greatly decreased, 1,600 deck class.

She was given a major refit at Hong Kong in 1957 and then again, but in Japan, in 1962. In the latter, she was fitted with improved gravity lifeboats.

Indian-born Neville Gordon worked aboard British India passenger ships in what came to be the company's twilight years, in the late 1950s and 1960s. 'BI, as we called it, was still "the firm" to work for. There was enormous prestige in being employed by British India. Their reputation carried over from earlier days. It was commonly said that the second highest paid official in colonial India was the managing director of Mackinnon, Mackenzie & Company, the Indian agents for BI. It was said he earned just a few rupees less than the British viceroy.'

Gordon served aboard several British India passenger ships in the 1960s, including the classic *Rajula*. 'On the Madras–Penang–Singapore run, business was still very busy in the sixties', he recalled. 'There were many Indians in Malaya and so there was lots of "commuting" to and from Penang. Singapore was duty-free and so Indians would make two, three and as many as eight voyages each year on the *Rajula*. In those days, deck class was one of the cheapest ways to travel. Passengers could bring along their own bedding. They could sleep up on the open decks or below deck, sometimes even in the ship's alleyways. They could buy two kinds of tickets, with and without food.'

Captain Ian Tompkins was a junior officer with British India in the 1960s. 'BI officers were a unique group. They were exceptionally proud and disciplined', he remembered. 'BI was one company during the Depression in the 1930s that never laid off anyone. They had superb cadet training, which bred huge fraternity. Of course, there were many impossible conditions and situations, especially on the Eastern passenger ships, but overall we actually lived like kings. Even the simplest occasions – such as a meal of curry and beer on the open deck in the Bay of Bengal – brings back happy memories for me. British India was a tremendously efficient company and all of their ships were kept in mint condition.'

Captain Tompkins also served aboard the *Rajula*. 'We carried Indian businessmen, traders and merchants in first and second classes, and lots of Indian workers for the Malaysian rubber plantations down in deck class. She also carried cargo including lots of Indian onions to Penang and Singapore. The *Rajula* was the best "sea ship" ever. She had fantastic stability. She was just magnificent. Myself, I was aboard her during two cyclones and she rode and handled beautifully. The steel in her hull was very solid and strong, and superior to the British steel used in the post-war passenger ships. Already a very old ship, she was just amazingly solid. Internally, she was classic – all wood and brass and polish.'

'On her return voyages to India, the cooks used to polish and scrub because there were less passengers', added Captain Tompkins. 'The *Rajula* had enormous deck space. The officers had cabins with doors that opened onto the deck and with enormously high bunks.'

End of the line! The *Rajula* was put up for sale in spring 1973, but not sold until October, going to the Shipping Corporation of India. Largely untouched, she was renamed *Rangat* and used on the Calcutta–Port Blair (Andaman Islands) service. It was all very short-lived, however. In little more than six months, on 2 May 1974, the well worn, very tired, forty-eight-year-old ship was laid up at Bombay. She was stripped of all fittings as well as her lifeboats. That fall, this unique, long-lasting ship was broken up at Bombay.

The *Rajula* in Kowloon Bay, Hong Kong, in an evocative scene dated 1957. (British India)

Different pricing: in 1926, the 8,478-grt *Rajula* cost almost £233,000 to build. (British India)

4

DILWARA (1936)

They are now long gone, of course, victims of changed economics and perhaps changed society. However, for decades they were a very popular part of British travel and, of course, British cruising. 'School ship cruising' provided holidays for youngsters, opportunities to go to sea, breathe the fresh air, sail with others and altogether have the educationally enriching experience of visiting faraway lands. History, geography and literature classes, to name a few, were easily blended as part of the onboard activities. Students from all walks of British life sailed and lived together, from posh boarding schools to tough inner cities. British India ran them as an adjunct to their Indian, East African and government trooping services beginning in the 1930s. Disrupted by the Second World War, these trips were not resumed until the early 1960s using several converted former peacetime troopships – the *Dilwara*, *Dunera* and *Devonia*. By the late 1960s the last two ships in this service were the improved and immensely popular *Nevasa* and *Uganda*.

In the mid-1930s the British government, or more specifically the Ministry of Transport in London, built a quartet of troopships – useful in peacetime, but more important in case of war. Commercial ship owners managed these vessels, however, and in doing so followed company nomenclature and on-board operational standards. British India had two of them, the 12,700-ton sisters *Dilwara* and *Dunera*. The third went to the Bibby Line, which sailed her as the *Devonshire*, while the fourth came under P&O and sailed as the *Ettrick* (but later sunk during the Second World War, in November 1942).

The 517-foot-long *Dilwara* was built by Barclay Curle & Company at Glasgow and was completed in January 1936. A motor ship with Doxford diesels, she was twin-screw and had a service speed of 13–14 knots. There was, it seemed, no need to be fast, but economical and practical. As built, quarters were arranged for 104 first class, 100 second class and up to 1,157 troops.

Used mostly on voyages to colonial outposts, there was one detour. In May 1937, she took part in King George VI's coronation fleet review off Portsmouth. By 1939 and into the early years of the war, she was used mostly on trooping voyages to South Africa as well as to and from the Suez. In April 1941

Between voyages: the *Dilwara* waiting at the Southampton Docks with the Booth Line's *Hildebrand* and the outer end of the Ocean Terminal in the background. (British India)

KUALA CRUISES

M. S.

KUALA LUMPUR

CRUISING TO

HONG KONG
JAPAN

Photos from the *Dilwara*'s second life as the *Kuala Lumpur*, a cruise ship for China Navigation Company. (Andrew Kilk Collection)

CRUISE IN LUXURY .. HAVE FUN ON BOARD

The public staterooms and saloon accommodation are designed for the maximum convenience when cruising. Drawing Room and Smoke Room, Dance Floor and Lounge, Swimming Pool and Lido form together a compact centre of shipboard life on the Promenade Deck, with its exceptional sheltered deck space. Please refer to the deck plans overleaf Meals are served in the Dining Saloon on the Shelter Deck, with two sittings at sea and special arrangements in port. Most of the cabins are on 'A' Deck where enquiries will be welcomed at the Bureau.

she called at Kalamata for the evacuation of Greece. During a 1942 refit she was converted to a landing ship, infantry, and was fitted with ten landing craft. By September she took part in the landings on Madagascar. She was in Burmese waters in the following year and suffered some mine damage. When the war ended, in the summer of 1945, she was trooping between Calcutta and Singapore, also between Penang and Bangkok as well as on voyages to Port Blair in the Andaman Islands.

The *Dilwara* underwent a ten-month, post-war refit at Barclay Curle. Some decking was rebuilt, the funnel was heightened and all the bunks replaced hammocks in the troop quarters. Her tonnage was revised to 12,555 and the berthing rearranged in improved conditions as 125 first class, 96 second class, 104 third class, with a maximum of 790 troops.

Used during the Korean War on voyages out to Japan, South Korea and other Far Eastern ports, the *Dilwara* continued thereafter in diverse, almost worldwide trooping. In August 1956, she had a special assignment: she took part in the Suez Canal landings for Anglo-French forces helping to resist the nationalization of the canal by the Egyptian president, Nasser.

No longer required for government service, the *Dilwara* was sold off in November 1960 to the China Navigation Company. Renamed *Kuala Lumpur*, she was refitted and altered at Hong Kong's Taikoo Dockyard. Her new role was mostly as a seasonal pilgrim ship to Jeddah and as an occasional cruise ship. Consequently, her quarters were rearranged yet again, this time for 243 first class and 1,669 pilgrims. She was an improved ship hereafter, with full air-conditioning, an outdoor pool and, thoughtfully, a mosque for her pilgrims.

Apart from her pilgrim voyages across the Indian Ocean, the otherwise aged ship found another career as a summer season Australian cruise ship. In September 1961, for example, she departed from Fremantle on the first of two forty-six-day cruises to the Far East. Afterward, she cruised from Sydney as well as Melbourne, and later under the banner of Kuala Cruises.

The ex-*Dilwara* carried on for another eleven years until December 1971, when she was decommissioned, sold to the Tung Cheng Steel Company and scrapped at Kaohsiung on Taiwan.

FLEET

Ship	Gross Tonnage	Ship	Gross Tonnage
AMRA	8,314	NEVASA	20,527
ARONDA	8 396	NOWSHERA	8,516
CANARA	7,024	NUDDEA	8,596
CARPENTARIA	7,268	NYANZA	8,513
CHAKDARA	7,132	OBRA	5,695
CHAKDINA	7,267	OKHLA	5,732
CHAKRATA	7,265	OLINDA	5,424
CHANDA	6,921	ORDIA	5,449
CHANDPARA	7,274	ORMARA	5,444
CHANTALA	7,551	ORNA	6,779
CHILKA	7,087	OZARDA	6,895
CHINDWARA	7,525	PACHUMBA	7,282
CHINKOA	7,102	PADANA	7,541
CHUPRA	6,957	PALAMCOTTA	6,662
CHYEBASSA	7,043	PALIKONDA	7,434
DARA	5,030	PEMBA	7,449
DARESSA	5,180	PENTAKOTA	6,672
DILWARA	12,555	PUNDUA	7,295
DUMRA	4,867	PURNEA	5,340
DUNERA	12,615	RAJULA	8,496
DWARKA	4,851	SANGOLA	8,646
FULTALA	4,589	SANTHIA	8,908
GARBETA	5,323	SIRDHANA	8,608
ITINDA	6,648	UGANDA	14,430
KAMPALA	10 304	UMARIA	6,835
KARANJA	10,294	URLANA	6,835
KENYA	14,464	WARLA	3,668
LANDAURA	7,289	WAROONGA	8,753
MOMBASA	2,213	WARORA	3,668
NARDANA	8,511	WOODARRA	8,753

BUILDING

Ship	Gross Tonnage	Ship	Gross Tonnage
BAMORA	6,750	BOMBALA	6,750
BANKURA	6,750	BULIMBA	6,750
BARPETA	6,750		

TANKERS BUILDING

Ship	Tons D.W	Ship	Tons D.W
ELLENGA	37,000	QUEDA	19,100
ELLORA	37,000	QUILOA	19,100
ERINPURA	37,000		

B·I STEAM NAVIGATION CO., LTD.

A list of the British India fleet, once one of Britain's largest shipping firms.

5

DUNERA (1937)

The British government began the gradual end of peacetime trooping by sea in the late 1950s. A sister ship to the *Dilwara*, the *Dunera*'s contract ended in 1960 and, while she might have been sold off or even scrapped, British India decided to revive its pre-war concept of educational cruising, mostly for British school children, with a small, separate adult section. She was refitted for £100,000 by Vickers-Armstrong at Hebburn-on-Tyne in 1960–61, upgraded from her troopship standard and restyled for as many as 1,028 passengers – 194 in the adult section, sometimes referred to as saloon class, and 834 children in dormitories. She was especially fitted with classrooms, lecture halls and, perhaps most notably, an outdoor swimming pool was added. She reappeared in British India colors and purposely had her masts shortened for transits of the Kiel Canal. She started educational cruising in the spring of 1961 and proved popular from the start. British India directors were encouraged to expand, and to add a second vessel.

'On these school cruises aboard the *Dunera*, we were actually terrified of carrying so many children', recalled Captain Ian Tompkins. 'We had "master mariners" attached to the school groups, mainly for safety but also for physical education. The children lived in dorms for as many as thirty while the teachers were mostly in cabins. We'd carry what seemed to be only a handful of adults in the former first class quarters. The children met local children at the different ports and this added to the experience. These educational cruises were popular and successful, but not tremendously profitable for BI. In the 1960s, it wasn't so expensive to run ships like the *Dunera*.'

By 1966 BI Educational Cruises was operating three ships – the *Dunera*, *Devonia* and *Nevasa*. Voyages included:

24 February: London to Algiers, Malta, Thessaloniki, Piraeus, return by air from Venice (fifteen days). Adult fares from £75.

8 March: to Venice by air, then Itea, Piraeus, Izmir, Naples, then return by air from Genoa (fifteen days). Adult fares from £64.

7 April: from London/Tilbury to Vigo, Tangier, Lisbon, Santander and return to London/Tilbury (fifteen days). Adult fares from £64.

22 April: from London/Tilbury to Copenhagen, Kiel Canal, Heligoland, Amsterdam, return to Avonmouth (ten days). Adult fares from £40.

13 May: from London/Tilbury to Trondheim, Andalsnes, Bergen, return to London/Tilbury (eleven days). Adult fares from £45.

28 June: from Greenock to Madeira, Casablanca, Lisbon, return to Greenock (fourteen days). Adult fares from £74.

The *Dunera*, also constructed by Barclay Curle, had been completed back in August 1937. Afterward and well into the war, in 1941, she trooped continuously – to South Africa, the Middle East, Singapore and Australia. During 1942 she was converted to a landing ship and later took part in the Majunga and subsequent Sicily landings. In August 1944 she had a noted task: she was the headquarters ship of the US Seventh Army for the invasion of the south of France. In May 1945 she took part in the reoccupation of Rangoon, then became the lead ship in the Malaysia landings and, following the end of war in the Pacific in August 1945, she resumed trooping, mostly between India and Malaya. In 1946 she carried Indian troops to occupied Japan and her return voyages included prisoners of war.

Like her earlier sister *Dilwara*, the *Dunera* was given a £1 million, ten-month, post-war refit (between March 1950 and May 1951). Still carrying 100 in first class and another 100 in second class, her troop quarters were reduced by 300 to a more comfortable peacetime standard, from 1,150 to 831. Thereafter, she was used for continuous trooping to Cyprus, Egypt, Ceylon and Malaya.

Captain Ian Tompkins served aboard her in 1957. 'Even as a peacetime trooper, the *Dunera* was all very regimental, very disciplined, very organized and very separate. The troops were in double-bunk accommodations and the military families in the cabin quarters. The passengers in first and second class had some amenities and recreations. There were records for dancing, quizzes and, in warm weather areas, a cinema on the open deck. The BI officers mixed with the passengers, but no others. She was, of course, a comparatively slow ship, making 12 knots at best. I also recall we had one special voyage during 1957 – we sailed from the UK to Christmas Island, carrying a contingent for the atomic testing being done there.'

In 1967, as the newly refitted *Uganda* was coming into educational cruise service, the thirty-year-old *Dunera* was made redundant. That November she was sold to Spanish shipbreakers and sailed to Bilbao for demolition.

Underway on a BI educational cruise, the *Dunera* at sea. (British India)

Another view of the *Dunera* in her cruising days. (British India)

6

DEVONIA (1939)

Since the *Dilwara* had already been sold off, in 1960, becoming the *Kuala Lumpur* for the Hong Kong-based China Navigation Company, British India looked to the surviving third sister of this group. Bibby's *Devonshire* had lost her trooping contract as well and so was up for sale. British India promptly bought her, refitted her and introduced her as the renamed *Devonia* in the spring of 1962. Built by Fairfield Shipbuilding & Engineering Company at Glasgow in 1939, she differed only slightly from the *Dunera* – the *Devonia* had a slim, raked funnel whereas the *Dunera* had a lower and wider funnel.

The 12,796-grt *Devonia* entered service in July 1939 with a voyage from Liverpool to Bombay. She was designed for up to 1,344 passengers – 104 first class, 90 second class and 1,150 troops. She was soon involved in the Second World War, and when her capacity was greatly expanded to as many as 4,000, she sailed on diverse voyages to South Africa, the Far East and within the Mediterranean. Notably, on 7 June 1944, the *Devonshire* and three other Bibby passenger ships, the *Cheshire*, *Lancashire* and *Worcestershire*, proceeded together down the English Channel carrying 10,000 troops between them for the Normandy Landings. Together, they were the first large passenger ships to do so for four years.

Resuming peacetime trooping, the 11,275-grt *Devonia* had a ten-month refit (April 1953–February 1954) with some alterations, but improvements especially to her troop quarters. She was reconfigured for 130 first class, 96 second class and a reduced 824 troops.

Made redundant by late 1961, Bibby sold the *Devonshire* to British India for £175,000 in the following January. She was promptly renamed *Devonia*, given a £100,000 refit at Barclay Curle in Glasgow for educational cruising (and which included the installation of a swimming pool on deck) and was thereafter listed as carrying 190 cabin (adult) passengers and 830 students (in dormitories). She had her first BI educational cruise that April.

As the newly refitted *Uganda* was coming into service in 1968, the *Devonia* was, like the *Dunera*, made redundant. She was sold to Italian scrappers in the fall of 1967 and was demolished at La Spezia that December.

With a slightly taller and more rounded funnel, the *Devonia* was the former Bibby Lines' *Devonshire*. (British India)

7

AMRA (1938) AND *ARONDA* (1941)

When David Andrews joined the British India Steam Navigation Company Limited in 1954, the British merchant fleet had some 6,000 ships and employed as many as 50,000 seamen. Trade was brisk almost everywhere in the world and the British Empire, though in its own Indian summer, was largely intact. Alone, BI had 136 ships. For Andrews, it was a career that went from freighters to passenger ships and finally to super tankers.

'My first ship was the freighter *Chantala*, which was also the company's training ship', he recalled. 'She carried up to forty cadets plus forty-four regular crew and twelve passengers. Altogether there was close to 100 onboard. We were on BI's UK–Australia service. Later, I went to BI's O Class freighters, which sailed between Bombay and Karachi and then to Malaysia, Hong Kong and Japan. In some areas, we were still on alert for mines left over from the Second World War. We carried all sorts of cargo – such as dates and cotton and even scrap metal from India to the Far East, and then returned with items such as sulfur, carbon, even sugar and newspapers.'

British India was an empire of sorts in itself. There were large company offices in Bombay, Calcutta, Singapore, Hong Kong, Mombasa and the main headquarters in London. There were British managers and either Indian or Chinese clerks in the overseas offices. David didn't return to his home in England for several years at a time. 'We worked on three-year contracts and then had leave and could go home for six months. We caught BI freighters going to and from the UK. But BI was like a big family. There was a BI Club in each port and these included sleeping accommodation. There were even ship-like restaurants in these clubs and the officers sat at the head tables and the juniors elsewhere. These were busy places, especially since there was always four or five British India ships in port.'

Even by 1960 British India had seventeen passenger ships. Andrews served on many of them. 'I was assigned to the little *Daressa* [5,180 tons and 586 passengers], which was used on the Bombay–Persian Gulf service. Our big trade was Indians traveling as deck class. Next, it was to the *Sangola* [8,647 tons and 1,415 passengers], which was then on the run between

India, Southeast Asia and the Far East. It was a long-haul service extending from Bombay all the way to Kobe and Yokohama. Again, we carried some passengers in first class, but mostly Chinese down in deck class.'

After serving aboard the larger *Karanja* and *Kampala*, David's next assignment was to the sisters *Amra* and *Aronda*. Each ship sailed on a different service. 'The *Amra* sailed between Karachi and Mombasa whereas the *Aronda* went around India, sailing between East and West Pakistan, between Chittagong and Karachi. Mostly, the Pakistani passengers were kept separate from the Indian passengers. These ships were very fast and, like most other BI ships of that time, were well built and heavily riveted.'

Captain Tompkins also served in the *Amra*. 'She was pre-war, but still [in the 1960s] a magnificent old ship. She had a very spacious bridge and what seemed to be miles of open, teak deck space. We carried lots of Indian business people to East Africa on the *Amra* and Indian workers, often with their families, in deck class. We also carried lots of Indian crews that would staff not only British India ships, but others from the Clan, Bank and Ellerman lines.'

'All BI passenger ships were very tidy, especially in cabin class', added Neville Gordon. 'The brass shined, the woods were polished, the bathrooms cleaned and the blowers worked. Little towels, starched and stiff, hung from loops in the bathrooms. There was always iced cold water in a carafe in the cabins.'

But times were changing. Decolonization of British territories was moving quickly by the early 1960s and almost immediately changed trading patterns for British-flag ships, passenger as well as freight. Then the huge P&O Company, owners of British India, took a stronger hold and decided to gradually phase out the BI passenger division. And finally, British seamen were becoming more expensive. Everything, it seemed, was changing. British India itself slowly downsized and all but disappeared completely by the mid-1980s. David Andrews, by now a captain, decided to make a change – he joined P&O-owned Trident Tankers. From the likes of the little 2,213-ton *Mombasa* and the 1,040-passenger *Karanja*, he was now in command of giant 200,000-ton tankers.

Built by Swan, Hunter & Wigham Richardson at Wallsend, the 8,314-grt *Amra* was the first of three sisters purposely designed for the India–Burma run. Launched on 29 April 1938, the 461 foot long ship was commissioned that November with a delivery voyage and carrying passengers from London to Calcutta via Suez. The trio were quite dated for their time as well as unique – they used coal and, down below, had mechanical coal stokers. Without doubt, and for as late as the 1940s, they were among the very last deep-sea ships to use coal. Rather expectedly, this eventually proved to be impractical as well as a nuisance. In the end, these ships had to be bunkered by coolies carrying one basket of coal at a time. The conversion of these ships, among the biggest transformations of their time in a South African port, was done at Durban beginning in 1950. Twin screw ships, they were intended for service speeds of 16 knots. The *Amra* was often said to be the most contemporarily decorated BI passenger ship of her day. In first class the lounge was done in weathered sycamore and the smoking room in Indian silver gray wood.

As the Second World War started in Europe in September 1939, the *Amra* – with berthing for as many as 2,636 passengers in all (45 first class, 110 second, 154 third and 2,327 deck) – continued for a time with her Calcutta–Rangoon sailings. In December 1940, however, she was officially called to war

Early days: the *Amra* at Durban in her original black hull. (British India)

duties and converted with 385 beds and with 107 medical staff to *Hospital Ship No 41*. Mostly, into 1943, she was used along the East African coast – from Somaliland to Mombasa and then down to Durban. Afterward, she was in Mediterranean waters – assisting, in July, in the Allied invasion of Sicily and then, in September, at Salerno. The *Amra* was released quickly in 1945 and was immediately refurbished for a return to her Calcutta–Rangoon service. Her accommodations were rearranged, however, for 222 cabin class and 737 deck class.

She almost made thirty years of service. She was sold for scrap in December 1966 and broken up at Keelung on Taiwan.

The second sister, the *Aska*, was completed in 1939, but, when little more than a year old, was bombed and sunk on 16 September 1940. Northbound from West Africa, she was approaching Liverpool at the time of the attack.

The building of the third sister, the *Aronda*, was underway in 1939 and the ship was due in the following year. Her construction abruptly stopped, however, when war began in September 1939. The British government had placed restraints on all non-essential ships. But after the *Aska* was lost in September 1940, work on the *Aronda* promptly resumed. She became a so-called 'essential ship'. Also built by Swan, Hunter & Wigham Richardson, she was completed in just months, being delivered in February 1941. Immediately pressed into service as an all-gray troopship, she went on to carry Australian forces to and from Ceylon and later Indian troops to and from Malaya.

The war and a resulting shortage of ships had prompted changes and so, after being decommissioned in the summer of

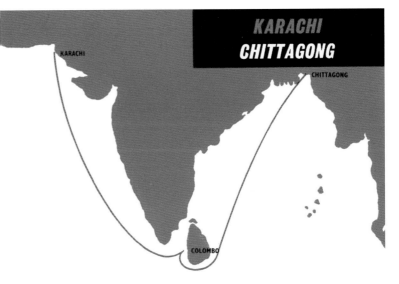

The Service	Monthly in both directions.
The Ship	" ARONDA "
Accommodation	First and Second Class, intermediate and unberthed.
Freight	General cargo with facilities for refrigerated cargo.
Ports of Call	Karachi, Colombo, Chittagong.
Schedule	Karachi to Chittagong—8 days.

The Karachi–Chittagong route.

The *Aronda* and *Amra* certainly looked more tropical with their all-white hull coloring. (British India)

1945, the *Aronda* was promptly fitted out as a passenger ship, but with a far smaller capacity for forty-four first class, twenty-two second class and twenty-eight in so-called interchangeable. In addition, she was certified for up to 1,800 unberthed passengers. Instead of the intended Rangoon service, she was initially used on the Bombay–Durban run. She 'carried on', as one former crew member recalled, until May 1963, when she was sold to Hong Kong shipbreakers. But her demolition was delayed. She went aground on outer Macao on 21 July, then had to be carefully refloated and so the scrapping of the *Aronda* did not begin until as late as mid-December.

'After the withdrawal of British India passenger routes and ships such as the *Amra* and *Aronda*, many Indians changed to the Shipping Corporation of India and then to airlines', recalled Neville Gordon. 'Ships such as the *Amra* and *Aronda* had been a huge training ground, in fact the only training group, for the managers, marine superintendents and especially crew members for the likes of the Shipping Corporation and the Scindia Lines. Other former BI crew, the stewards and waiters, found work in hotels.'

8

KAMPALA (1946) AND *KARANJA* (1948)

'For the most part, the *Kampala* and *Karanja* were identical sister ships. They were built after the war, in the late 1940s, but from blueprints from the pre-war *Kenya* of 1930', noted Harry Atkinson. 'There were heavy war losses and so far fewer ships were about when the war ended in 1945. The British government insisted on quickly restoring these British India passenger links and so gave priority to the construction of all the BI passenger ships. New designs would have taken over a year, however. So to avoid waiting for new drawings and plans, British India pulled out pre-war sketches and plans. Consequently, 1946–48 ships were built to 1930 designs. In all, however, they were charming ships, very solidly built and with superb turbine machinery.'

Apart from the London-based *Kenya* and *Uganda*, these 10,300 tonners were the 'stars' of British India's overseas passenger fleet. Both built by Alexander Stephen & Sons at Glasgow, the 507 foot long *Kampala* came first, being launched on 11 December 1946; the *Karanja* followed fourteen months later, on 10 March 1948. They were actually planned and using those slightly reworked pre-war designs even before the war officially ended, in November 1944, and then formally ordered (from Alexander Stephen) a month later. The *Kampala* was laid down four months after VJ Day, in December 1945. There was to have been something of a ceremony for the launch of the £1,100,000 *Kampala*. Lady Currie, the chairman's wife, named her with King Mutesa II of Buganda present, but fog on the Clyde was so thick that actual launching was impossible. The naming took place while the ship remained in her building slip and then was rather unceremoniously launched the next day. Designed to carry both European as well as large numbers of Indian passengers, these ships were based on designs of a previous, similar British India pair of sisters, the *Karanja* and *Kenya* of 1930–31. Neither reappeared after the Second World War, however. The *Karanja* was sunk in the war, in November 1942; the *Kenya* was eventually sold off, went through several name changes and finally became the *Castel Felice* for Italy's Sitmar Line (and sailed, often in the Europe–Australia migrant and tourist trade, until scrapped in 1970).

Driven by steam turbines, these twin-screw sisters could manage 16 knots as a standard service speed. Like the subsequent *Kenya* and *Uganda*, they each had five cargo holds, mostly for general cargo, but some refrigerated space as well.

The 'new' *Karanja* and her sister were soon recognized for having very comfortable first and second class quarters. In first class especially, they had well-fitted and decorated public rooms, an outdoor pool, and drew high praises for, according to one travel guide in the 1950s, their 'excellent cuisine and fine Indian service'.

They were the primary passenger ships on the busy India–Africa run. They sailed on timely schedules from Bombay to Porebunder, Bedibunder, Karachi, over to the Seychelles, then to Mombasa (where passengers could connect to the *Kenya* or *Uganda*), Zanzibar, Dar-es-Salaam, Beira, Lourenco Marques and Durban. The ships were certified for up to 2,441 passengers each – 60 first class, 180 second class and 1,400 deck class was the official listing, but the actual numbers varied over the years. Suitable to such high numbers, each ship had no less than twenty-six lifeboats and two motor launches. There were two deluxe first class cabins with private baths, but all others used public facilities. 'The *Karanja* was the most superior of all BI's Eastern passenger ships', in Captain Tompkins's opinion. 'She was even superior to her sister ship, the *Kampala*. Generally, the *Karanja* had better on-board configuration.'

There were periodic changes in schedule, diversions and even charters. The *Kampala* was chartered to the Indian government in the spring of 1948, as an example. She carried over 1,600 Muslim evacuees from Bombay to Karachi and then reversed from Karachi with 2,100 Hindu refugees. In reverse, on occasion, BI chartered other passenger ships to assist or fill in on the busy India–East Africa run. These included the Mogul Line's *Mohammedi* and *Mozzafari* (built in 1947–48, 7,000 tons and carrying approximately 1,500 passengers each). In 1955 the pair adopted, like the other BI passenger ships, the all-white hull coloring.

Beginning in 1954, David Andrews was a crew member with British India. One of his favorite assignments in the 1950s and 1960s was sailing between India, the Seychelles and then ports in East and South Africa on board the popular sister ships *Karanja* and *Kampala* (10,300 tons). 'We'd carry South African passengers, businessmen and even tourists, in first class and Indian workers in deck class. The South Africans often used these ships for their holidays – sailing from Durban up to Mombasa, then spending time ashore in a hotel and then catching the returning ship back to Durban. The *Karanja* and *Kampala* worked on four-week roundtrip schedules. They were lovely ships for both passengers and for crew. They weren't air-conditioned, but we were soon used to the heat and also had big fans in our cabins. As officers, we were expected to learn Hindi and always carried a language book.'

Neville Gordon also served aboard the *Kampala* and *Karanja* on the India–East Africa run and added, 'There were many Indian expatriates in South and East Africa. This formed a great part of our business. We also carried lots of tourists to and from the Seychelles from both East Africa as well as Bombay. Until the 1960s, BI ships were the only means of transport to and from the Seychelles. There was no airport there. Cargo was also an important component to these ships – they carried spices, cotton, clothing and general cargo from Bombay; from East Africa, there were spices, fruits and what

Almost stately looking, the *Karanja* as built in 1948. (British India)

we called "finished cargo". We also carried goods that were trans-shipped from the Far East.'

'In first class, on board the *Karanja* and *Kampala*, we carried civil servants, wealthy Britons (called Pakka Sahib), tourists, some students and visitors. We also carried lots of inter-port passengers along the East African coast', added Gordon. 'In first class, these ships were run to excellent organization and to great efficiency. And with style as well. In first class, it was British cuisine with an Indian accent. Every Sunday, we served Roast Beef with Yorkshire Pudding, Country Capon and Kedgeree [spiced rice]. The tables were set with white linen and sparkling silver. There were four o'clock afternoon teas with violin music, and dancing on deck to an Indian band in the evenings. The officers always dressed for dinner. Both the *Kampala* and *Karanja* had forced-air ventilation in first and second class, and had a portable swimming pool for days at sea.'

'It was quite different aboard the *Karanja*, *Kampala* and the other BI ships that carried deck class', added Brian Gregory. 'It was a contrast – up in first and second class, British items appeared on the menus along with cakes and cucumber sandwiches for four o'clock teas; in deck class, in varied robes, costumes and sometimes caps, thousands of chappatties were produced instead for the Indian passengers as well as a vast array of foods prepared by themselves.'

Every fall for some fifteen years, Harry Atkinson and wife traveled from London to Mombasa and then on to the Seychelles; they made the reverse voyage in spring. 'For many years, we traveled only aboard the *Kenya* and *Uganda* to and

The very popular Bombay–Africa service of British India.

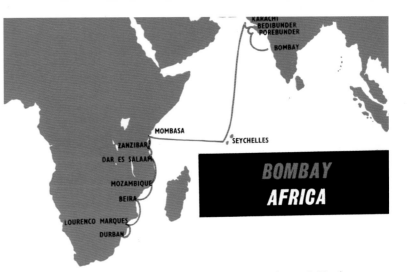

BOMBAY AFRICA

The Service	Two sailings a month from Bombay and Mombasa, monthly sailings to and from South Africa.
The Ships	" AMRA ", " KAMPALA ", " KARANJA "
Accommodation	" KAMPALA " and " KARANJA ", First Class, including de luxe cabins, Second Class, Third Class. " AMRA ", Saloon Class and Third Class.
Freight	General and refrigerated cargo.
Ports of call	Bombay, Porebunder, Bedibunder, Karachi, Seychelles, Mombasa, Zanzibar, Dar es Salaam, Mozambique, Beira, Lourenco Marques, Durban.
Schedule	Bombay to Dar es Salaam—9 days (" AMRA "). Bombay to Durban—21 days (" KAMPALA ", " KARANJA ").

B·I SERVICES

Busy day: the *Karanja* loading at Bombay. (British India)

An aerial view of the *Karanja* in her white hull coloring adopted from 1955. (British India)

from London', he recalled. 'We had business along the East African coast, at Dar-es-Salaam, Zanzibar and Durban, and so we lived aboard the ship. In those days, in the 1960s, we also did lots of business in the Seychelles and so we would connect, once or twice on the same day, from the *Kenya* or *Uganda* to the *Kampala* or *Karanja*. We loved being aboard ships, especially ships of British India, and so it was all very convenient.'

'In the 1950s Indian laborers could cross the Indian Ocean to East Africa in deck class for about $100', recalled Atkinson. 'They'd feed themselves and take their own bed roll. Often, they'd put all their possessions in a 50-gallon oil drum and roll it along the quayside and then onto the ship. They also sometimes traveled with tin trunks.'

These two sisters tended to be very punctual. 'When, say, the *Kampala* was due at 0600 at the Beira pilot station, she arrived at 0600', added Atkinson. 'There were the occasional incidents, even close calls, of course. I remember when the *Karanja* was almost lost. Late one night at Mombasa when cargo was being loaded on board, it was done incorrectly, unevenly. The ship gradually began to list. The captain fell out of bed. The ship had a 30 degree list. She started to take on water through some open portholes along the lower decks. Water rushed in and the captain went down personally to close the open ports and so saved the ship from sinking. Also, the *Karanja* ran into a tidal wave, in August 1950, but fortunately was undamaged.'

It was all changing by the 1960s, however. According to Harry Atkinson, 'The India–East Africa run was gradually becoming a one-way trade – Indians and Pakistanis returning home from East Africa. There were less and less passengers coming from India. Air links had developed from Nairobi to Bombay and, locally, from Nairobi down to Durban. Soon, even the deck passengers could afford to travel by air. Eventually, the Shipping Corporation of India took over this run with ships such as the *State of Bombay* and *State of Haryana*, and the new *Harshivadana*, built in India, but with technical aid from Britain.'

The *Karanja* was specially refitted in 1969–70. She sailed to Singapore and was given a major refit and renewal at the Keppel Shipyard. Her berthing was now revised as 493 cabin class and 750 deck. 'She was updated and even had video entertainment in the public rooms. It was all fed from some central control', added Atkinson.

The *Kampala* was made redundant by 1971, however, and, after making a voyage up to Hong Kong that July, was sold to the China Steel Corporation for demolition. She reached Kaohsiung on Taiwan on 25 July for scrapping.

The *Karanja* finally closed out the Bombay–East Africa service in 1976, then was laid up at Bombay and finally sold that July to the Shipping Corporation of India. Renamed *Nancowry*, she was placed on the Madras–Port Blair, Andaman Islands service. She was scrapped in 1988.

Threesome: a trio of British India passenger ships seen together at Mombasa in 1963 – the *Uganda* on the left, the *Karanja* in the center, and the *Kenya* on the right. (British India)

Securely alongside: the *Karanja* at Kilindini, Kenya, in 1963. (British India)

P&O's passenger-cargo liner *Chitral* (left) and the *Karanja* at Durban, in a view dated 1969. (British India)

9

SANGOLA (1947), *SIRDHANA* (1947) AND *SANTHIA* (1950)

Just like the *Kampala* and *Karanja*, this smaller, 8,700-grt trio of near-sisters were also part of British India's large post-war rebuilding program. They too were quite purposeful. 'Ships such as the *Sangola*, *Sirdhana* and *Santhia* not only carried Indian passengers, but Chinese passengers as well, between Singapore and ports in the Far East', remembered Neville Gordon. 'There were also Bengalis out from Chittagong and then back to Calcutta.'

Expectedly, cargo greatly added to the revenues as well. 'We transported raw goods from India, especially bales and bales of cotton', added Gordon. 'From the Far East, there were textiles and large consignments of cheap manufactured goods – the likes of plastic umbrellas, transistor radios and shoes. Occasionally, we also carried crated Japanese automobiles.'

Captain Tompkins added, 'We carried Indian laborers to Singapore and Hong Kong, and then mostly businessmen only to Japan. For cargo, I remember lots of textiles going out and returning to India with manufactured goods. This Far East passenger service was actually the first to dry up, however. It was replaced by cargo ships.'

The 479-foot-long *Sangola* was the first of this trio, being built by Barclay Curle at Glasgow, and entered service in June 1947. She cost £1,100,000 to build. As completed, she had quarters for 21 first class, 34 second class 'A', 30 second class 'B' and 1,500 deck class passengers.

The *Sangola* nearly met a premature end, however, when, on 1 July 1954, she went aground at Calcutta on Hirajunj Sand, Moyapur. The bow was firmly ashore with the stern riding up and down with the changing tide. Oil from ruptured pipes floated in the engine room and then had to be piped out to reduce the risk of fire. When finally salvaged and fully refloated after seven days, on 8 July, the bottom of the hull was found to be badly damaged. She might have been written off as a loss, but fourteen months of repairs seemed economically viable for the six-year-old ship. During the repairs, she was cut in two, a new centre section was fitted and then fore and aft sections then rejoined. When the *Sangola* resumed sailings in November 1954, she also had somewhat revised berthing arrangements in her third class for 335 berthed, while deck class was reduced from 1,500 to 995.

There were more troubles for the 15-knot *Sangola* in 1956 when she had propeller damage and then had to have extended repairs at the Whampoa Dockyard at Hong Kong. Her days ended when she was broken up in Japan in 1963.

The *Sirdhana* differed in that it was built by the Swan, Hunter & Wigham Richardson yard at Newcastle. She arrived six months after the first sister, in December 1947, and sailed in her intended Calcutta–Japan 'mail service' for the next fourteen years. In the spring of 1961 following the loss of the *Dara*, she was moved to the Bombay–Gulf run. Her berthing numbers were expectedly changed to suit that service: 21 first class, 32 second class, 30 intermediate, 333 berthed and 987 deck class. The *Sirdhana* continued until sold for scrap to the Taiwanese in August 1973. 'I seem to recall that the *Sirdhana* did a "home run" to the UK and Rotterdam via Suez in her final years', recalled Captain Tompkins. 'I also recall some perspective buyers coming aboard and who wanted to convert her to a sheep carrier. Obviously, this never materialized.'

The third sister, the *Santhia*, arrived three years after the first two, being launched in June 1950 and then completed that November. She might have been seriously damaged or even lost when the KPM's *Kaliangat* dragged her anchor and fell downstream onto the *Santhia* in February 1953. A barge was interposed between the two ships as a fender and this quickly prevented far more serious damage.

In 1962 the *Santhia* was rerouted and made some Bombay–East Africa voyages. 'The *Santhia* was the nicest ship that BI owned, in my opinion – she was charming, friendly and cozy', recalled

The more distant Bay of Bengal service. (British India)

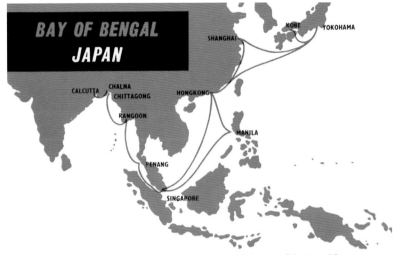

The Service	Approximately three-weekly between Calcutta and Japan. Monthly between East Pakistan and Japan
The Ships	" SANGOLA ", " SANTHIA ", and 3 cargo vessels.
Accommodation	First and Second Class, intermediate, bunked and unberthed in " SANGOLA " and " SANTHIA "
Freight	General cargo with refrigerated space available in " SANGOLA " and " SANTHIA "
Ports of Call	Calcutta, East Pakistan, Burma, Malaya, Hong Kong and Japan, calling at Manila and other intermediate ports as required Cargo vessels call Shanghai inwards to India.
Schedule	Calcutta to Japan—26 days.

Trading to the Far East: the *Sirdhana* at Hong Kong. (British India)

Captain Tompkins. 'Used on the Far East service to Hong Kong and Japan, she occasionally appeared on the East African run as relief for the *Karanja* or *Kampala*. I recall her carrying lots of cobra from the Seychelles to India and galvanized iron pipe from India to East Africa. She also carried, from Bombay, lots of sanitary ware such as sinks and toilets, builders' supplies and roofing tiles.'

With changes in trading requirements, the *Santhia* was sold in 1967 to the Shipping Corporation of India and renamed *State of Haryana* for further Bombay–East Africa service. In 1974, she moved onto the Calcutta–Port Blair in the Andaman Islands service. Time was running out for her, however. In November 1976 she suffered a serious boiler collapse. Extensive repairs

Brand new: the *Santhia* on trials. (British India)

At anchor: the *Sangola* at Hong Kong. (British India)

Another evocative view, but of the *Santhia* in her all-white coloring. (British India)

were impractical and instead the twenty-six-year-old ship was laid up at Bombay. A short time later, in February, she was sold to local shipbreakers.

10

DUMRA (1946), *DWARKA* (1947), *DARA* (1948) AND *DARESSA* (1950)

Smallest of all the immediate post-war replacement passenger ships, this 4,800-ton quartet was designed purposely for the India–Persian Gulf trade. Named *Dumra*, *Dwarka*, *Dara* and *Daressa*, these little 'work horses' all but disappeared in the vast British-flag passenger ship fleet of the 1950s. Three were built by Barclay Curle at Glasgow: the 4,867-grt *Dumra* almost immediately after the war, being completed in December 1946; the *Dara* in June 1948; and, in over four years since the first sister, the *Daressa* in June 1950. The second of the pair, the 399-foot-long *Dwarka*, completed in June 1947, came from Swan, Hunter & Wigham Richardson's yard at Newcastle.

The 14-knot *Daressa*, actually the largest of the four at 5,180 tons, was actually thought to be intended for India–East Africa service, but this never happened.

Almost typical to British India sister ships and near sisters, details and some arrangements for these ships varied. Specifically, numbers of passengers differed. Suffice to say, the *Dumra*, as the lead ship, was built to carry, almost like the dozen berths onboard a freighter, 13 in first class, 41 in second class and up to 1,537 unberthed or deck class. There were any number of changes in the berthing arrangements over the years. In 1952 the *Dumra* was relisted as having 20 berths in first class, 30 in second, but still a great number in deck class. By 1962 the *Daressa* had a refit and showed 90 one class in cabins and then 659 deck passengers on so-called 'short voyage fair', 578 on 'short voyage foul' or 271 during 'long voyage'. The last of the ships, the *Dwarka*, was finally listed in 1979 as carrying 52 cabin class, 534 berthed in deck class and 533 on deck. The actual number of crew varied, but numbered 130 in the early years.

These ships worked what was called the Express Gulf service for all of their lives – sailing from Bombay and Karachi to Gwadur, Muscat, Dubai, Umm Said, Bahrain, Bushire, Kuwait, Khorramshahr and Basrah. It was a major link, busy and very popular as well as profitable for many years.

The use of an all-white hull was first tried aboard these D Class ships in 1955. It was quickly seen as successful, reducing the onboard temperatures by 7 to as much as 10 degrees. This

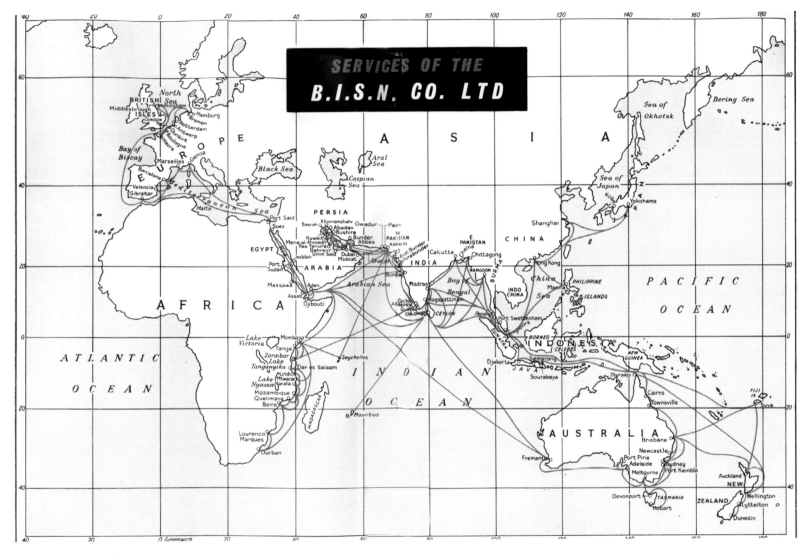

A map of British India services, dated 1955.

was notably beneficial to the ships' cabin passengers. Promptly, it was done to all BI passenger ships with the exception of the little *Mombasa*.

'When tied up in ports, ships such as these could be especially unbearable', remembered Captain Tompkins. 'Places like Basrah could be 100 degrees day after day. Just about everyone slept out on deck. In later years, only the ship's hospital and the first class restaurant were air-conditioned. Like almost all of BI's post-war passenger ships [with the exception of the *Kenya* and *Uganda*], ships such as *Dumra*, *Dwarka*, *Dara* and *Daressa* were really built in a hurry. They were of pre-war design and post-war creation. Most of them were good, sound ships, however. They were built on priority status by the British government, the Indians and BI itself to restore important services and vital links. After construction, none of the four ever returned to the UK. They did their dry docking and refits at Bombay.'

'We sometimes called them the "Four D's"', recalled Captain Ian Tompkins. 'On their Gulf sailings, we had mostly business people, all Indians and rarely Europeans, in first and second class. Sometimes they would be traveling with their families, even servants and ayahs for the children. In third class, we had Indian laborers mostly and the occasional religious pilgrim. It was "rough accommodation" – open deck spaces, public toilets and cooking facilities. Otherwise, these passengers brought their own bedding as well as cooking and eating utensils. Overall, and while massed together with little space and even less privacy, these third class passengers were pleasant and disciplined. There

**BOMBAY
PERSIAN GULF**

The Service	Approximately every 6 days in both directions.
The Ships	" DARA ", " DARESSA ", " DUMRA ", " DWARKA ", " SIRDHANA "
Accommodation	First and Second Class, and unberthed.
Freight	General and refrigerated cargo.
Ports of Call	Connecting Bombay and Karachi with Persian Gulf ports, terminating at Basrah.
Schedule	Bombay to Basrah in 11 days. Basrah to Bombay in 9 days.

**B·I
SERVICES**

Another very popular and busy route: the Bombay Persian Gulf service.

were the odd, nasty incidents – such as stabbings and even suicides. Up until the early 1960s we still had full loads in both directions on this Express Gulf service. Still at its peak, there was virtually a BI ship a day at Bombay.'

'I recall the *Daressa* particularly being singled out and called the "Queen of the Gulf" because she had more cabins than the other three sisters', added Captain Tompkins. 'In deck class there were bunks in the lower 'tween decks and dormitories for about 100 each. But often even those who booked a bunk still brought aboard their own bedding. We also sold tickets with and without food. There were separate Muslim and Hindu galleys. We also had virgins' cages, real barred cage dormitories with regular patrols at night, so that the unattached ladies were kept safe.'

Cargo was expectedly part of this service as well. 'We carried clothing, manufactured goods and – the biggest cargo – textiles', added Captain Tompkins. 'We were much lighter on the return voyages to Bombay. Often, we had large consignments of dates. They were very much "working ships" – and, as I recall, also cockroach-infested ships.'

'British India had great organization and a huge fleet still by the late 1950s. The company was split between the "home people" [London] and the "coast people" [Bombay and Calcutta]. There were separate superintendents in Bombay and in Calcutta. On ships such as the *Dwarka*, we'd have three weeks out and a week home. There were BI clubs in Bombay and in Calcutta. But things were also beginning to change by the late 50s. The old order was beginning to change. It was the start of a great transition, but always a very civilized and well mannered transition. The Indians were taking over more and more. We had more Indian officers on the ships themselves. There was very little antagonism or bitterness between the British and the Indians – but the writing was clearly on the wall.'

Unintentionally, the *Dara* was the first to go. She caught fire after an on-board bomb explosion while sailing off Dubai on 10 April 1961. The incident made headline news around the world and was a harsh blow not only to British India, but to Britain and British influence in the Middle East. The burning ship was quickly abandoned. Three Royal Navy frigates responded, fought the blaze and finally brought the fire under control. She was later taken in tow, bound for Bahrain, by the deep-sea tug *Ocean Salvor*. Unfortunately, the empty, badly scorched ship sank two days later. The death tolls were high – 174 passengers, 14 Dubai shore staff and 24 crew.

'The *Dara* incident was, in ways, a great turning point for British India and its passenger services East of Suez', added Captain Tompkins. 'It was the beginning of the end.'

As trading conditions changed and passenger loads decreased, the *Daressa* was withdrawn in 1964 and, in August, was sold to the Marivic Navigation Company, flying the Liberian flag and an arm of the fast-growing Greek-owned Chandris Company, which had very successful liner services between Europe and Australia, and who were then also developing a separate cruise division. The *Daressa* was bought purposely for this latter operation, called Chandris Cruises. Chandris owners, managers and especially marine staff much favored ex-American and ex-British passenger ships, primarily because of their solid, well made construction. They then rebuilt them with double or even triple capacities. Afterward, they were often reintroduced as all but 'brand new' ships.

A compact little ship: the 5,000-grt *Daressa* on trials in 1950. (British India)

At anchor: the *Dumra* on a rare visit to Hong Kong. (World Ship Society)

The *Daressa* was renamed *Favorita*, taken to Greece (near Piraeus and where Chandris had its ship conversion operation) and was to be converted to carry 600 all first class passengers. It was planned that she would sail the Eastern Mediterranean, from Piraeus to the Greek islands and Turkey, for eight months of the year; the remainder, in deep winter, would be spent in the Caribbean. But upon further inspection, plans for the *Favorita* were shelved. She sat idle for the next four years. She would not become a gleaming, all-white Chandris cruise ship but, in 1968, was sold off to Singapore-based Guan Guan Shipping Company. Renamed *Kim Hwa*, she ran passenger sailings around Far East ports until she retired in 1974. That July she was sold to Hong Kong shipbreakers.

The third sister, the *Dumra*, remained with British India until 1972, when she was chartered to Damodar Bulk Carriers Ltd and then, in 1976, was bought outright. She was laid up at Bombay in May 1978 and finally, with no further use coupled with increased age and worn out machinery, she was sold in the following February to Bombay scrappers.

The *Dwarka* seemed to endure. 'There was just enough trade left by the late 1970s to support the aging *Dwarka* on the Bombay–Gulf run', noted Captain Tompkins.

When the *Dwarka* – that hard-worked little ship that sailed the Persian Gulf passenger and freight trades for well over three decades – went to the scrappers in 1982, a curtain came down with her. She was the last of an old breed of 'working' British passenger ships. Alone, she was also something of a final link to the Empire – to the British Imperial Raj, a colonial India, of high commissioners and their entourages, and to an age of travel that would seem purely antiquated compared to today's

jetcraft and cruise ship standards. While the *Uganda* was still sailing and the former *Karanja* was sailing as the Indian *Nancowry*, the demise of the *Dwarka* signaled to many the end of what was British India and those long-ago Eastern passenger services.

The *Dwarka*, named for a small town on India's northwest coast, carried a near incredible range of travelers over the years. Sometimes there were sheiks and their parties of family, servants and even bodyguards, who altogether occupied entire blocks of staterooms in the otherwise small, intimate first class section. They sometimes dished out the likes of gold watches as tips. One of these Eastern royals once came aboard with enough personal cargo to fill an entire hold, plus a personal cook, servants, his pet falcons and an entire string of hunting dogs. One crew member aboard the *Dwarka* recalled, 'Although a small, very unpretentious ship, we played host to princes, corseted maharajas and entertained regal entourages with all the pomp and circumstance of the era.'

There was another side to the passenger service of the *Dwarka*. Over the years she endured several riots among those souls in the lower-deck, 'unberthed' spaces. Several passengers – somewhere computed at the rate of three per year – went over the side to grisly suicides. Usually, they were despondent after finding that their relocation in one of the Gulf states was not the promised land or well paying job they expected. Others, deep in debt in their original homes, could not face returning after the promise of a new home or job elsewhere had collapsed. This deck class was usually well booked. Such quarters allowed these passengers to all but drag along all their luggage and other goods without paying excess air freight or simply because

Between sailings: the *Dumra* moored at Bombay. (British India)

The tragic destruction of the *Dara* in April 1961. (British India)

Last survivor: dressed in flags, the *Dwarka* was the last of the four D Class passenger-cargo ships to survive. (British India)

their sponsors refused to pay for air tickets altogether. Also, the *Dwarka* had been the executor of many repatriation orders.

The *Dwarka* sailed with a full staff of 122 – a figure actually somewhat higher than would apply for a similar-sized passenger vessel in today's cost-conscious cruise industry. The duties of the crew ranged from supervising the Eastern kitchens, which, among other accomplishments, churned out as many as 4,000 chapattis (whole wheat bread baked in a special clay oven) a day, to arranging for the showing of films in the lounge for cabin passengers and on deck for the others.

The trade continued to decline. While some voyages averaged 500–600 passengers, others dropped to a scant 100.

Her engines, barely producing a sluggish 11–12 knot sailing speed, had become museum pieces – or as one engineer called them, 'an old sewing machine'. Chief engineer John Smith was asked about his problems on the *Dwarka*. He pondered and then responded, 'No, just one problem: how to keep the damn thing going!' Another problem for the ship's mechanical side was that parts were simply unavailable. In those final years, in the late 1970s, everything had to be made by hand by a specialist British firm and then shipped to Bombay. A BBC television documentary on the *Dwarka*, made in 1979 and which stressed the ship's unique, historic status, prompted scads of journalists – from as far afield as Montreal and Tokyo – to make one last sentimental journey aboard what was called 'the old girl'. She also made a cameo appearance in the film *Gandhi*, released in 1982. Her final crew members were reassigned within the P&O fleet, some to the far larger and fancier passenger liners of P&O Cruises.

The thirty-five-year-old *Dwarka* was broken up at Karachi in May 1982.

A poetic scene of the charming *Dwarka* at Karachi. (British India)

11

MOMBASA (1950)

'She was a beautiful little ship, almost like a large yacht', remembered regular BI passenger Harry Atkinson. 'She was built purposely for the cashew nut trade out of Mtwara.' The little *Mombasa*, the first of two coastal passenger ships, was launched at the Henry Robb & Company shipyard at Leith in October 1949. At a mere 2,200 gross tons, she was designed to carry as few as 8 first class passengers (in quarters with a small lounge and a small dining room shared with the officers), 16 second class and up to 250 deck passengers. She also had three holds for cargo and, using British Polar diesels, was designed for a service speed of 12.5 knots (she actually made nearly 14 knots on her trials). She cost just under £300,000 to build and later set off on a long, slow maiden voyage, from London out to Mombasa via the Suez, that altogether took over six weeks.

The 266-foot-long *Mombasa* was designed purposely as a separate link, with the connecting, larger BI ships, between Mombasa, Tanga, Dar-es-Salaam, Kilwa, Lindi and Mtwara. For some years she was the only link between these mostly remote ports. Rare deviations included traveling to and from Bombay for periodic repairs and surveys.

According to David Andrews, 'The best assignments at BI were on the little passenger ship *Mombasa*, which sailed only along the East African coast between Mombasa and Mtwara. She was often back in Mombasa, where many BI officers had wives and families, within a week to ten days. The other prime assignment was the BI tugboat *Alusha*, which towed BI's barges along the East African coast.'

Although she carried over 200,000 passengers in ten years, the always mechanically troublesome *Mombasa* was the first of the post-war passenger ships to leave the BI fleet. Along with staffing problems, this little ship had become too expensive to operate. Retired in August 1960, she was laid up (at Kilindini) for well over a year before being sold, in October 1961, to Pakistani buyers, the Crescent Shipping Lines, for £130,000 and renamed *Kareem*. Her new career was rather brief, however. She was scrapped within five years in 1966.

Coastal passenger ship: the little *Mombasa* was created for a local service along the East African coast. (British India)

12

MTWARA (1951)

BI planned for a second East African coastal liner, the 2,696-grt *Mtwara*, which was launched at Henry Robb's yard at Leith in August 1950. She was commissioned early in the following year, in February, and with a slightly greater capacity than the otherwise similarly sized *Mombasa*. The *Mtwara* could carry up to 26 first class passengers, 40 second class and 250 deck.

The dramatic failure of the Groundnut Scheme in the early 1950s made the 298 foot long *Mtwara* superfluous almost from the start, however. Instead, BI managers were resourceful – they placed her in Persian Gulf service, from Karachi to Muscat,

Bandar Abbas, Shahjah and Dubai. Alternately, she was used in Bay of Bengal service out of Calcutta. She was misplaced altogether, however, and within two years, by March 1953, she was sold to Saigon owners for French-Indochinese coastal sailings as the *Ville de Haiphong*. That service was unsuccessful as well and within another three years, by 1956, she became the *Navarino* for Chilean owners. She was based at Valparaiso and again used for coastal service. By the early 1990s she was reportedly still about, but in use by the Chilean Navy.

13

LEICESTERSHIRE (1949)

Business on the 'Home Line' service between the UK and East Africa was booming, no doubt prompted by the possible great prosperity of the Groundnut Scheme in Tanganyika, and so additional passenger tonnage was needed in the early 1950s. The aged M Class ships were valiantly still serving out of London, but there was also massive port congestion along East Africa. There were increasing delays and changes in schedules and so these older ships could not keep up with demand. With the *Kenya* and *Uganda* coming on line in 1951–52, British India looked for help and found it with another British shipowner, the Bibby Line. BI chartered Bibby's combination passenger-cargo ship *Leicestershire* for what came to be five years of service on the East African route.

Built in 1949 by Fairfield of Glasgow, this 8,992-grt ship and her sister *Warwickshire* were created for Bibby's Liverpool–Suez–Rangoon service. They were in fact Bibby's last newly built passenger-cargo liners. That trade was waning, however, and so a charter to British India might have been a welcome alternative. After having collided with a tanker, the *British Jaguar*, while in the Suez Canal in April 1950, the *Leicestershire* needed months of repairs before joining BI's London–East Africa service that August.

The *Leicestershire*, while not renamed but repainted with BI funnel colors, was something of a good match to the M Class ships with their approximate 175 one-class berths. The 498-foot-long *Leicestershire* could carry seventy-six passengers, all in one class. Typically, there were two public rooms, a dining room and all but two special cabins were without private bathroom facilities. She did, however, have an outdoor swimming pool, the only one on the British India's London–East Africa run of 1950, just before the new *Kenya* and *Uganda*.

With passenger operations on the East African service becoming somewhat less demanding, the charter of the *Leicestershire* ended in March 1955. She was returned to the Bibby Line and resumed Liverpool–Rangoon passenger sailings until 1964 and then, rather briefly, was downgraded to a twelve-passenger freighter on the same run. She and her sister, the *Warwickshire*, were sold to Greek buyers, the Typaldos Lines, in 1966 and rebuilt as large passenger ferries for the Aegean islands service.

Bibby Line's *Leicestershire*, built for the UK–Burma run, did a stint under charter to British India. Her funnel colors were changed for the duration of the charter. (Gillespie-Faber Collection)

The *Leicestershire*, which became the *Heraklion*, carrying up to 1,450 passengers and 200 autos, had a most tragic ending. During a fierce storm in the Aegean on 8 December 1966 she sank within fifteen minutes and with the loss of 241 lives.

The incident made worldwide headlines. In the inquiries that followed, it was found that she was unsafely loaded; this led to the closing of the Typaldos Lines by the Greek government. The entire Typaldos passenger fleet was seized.

14

KENYA (1951)

When built in the very early 1950s, the 14,400-grt *Kenya* and her sister *Uganda* were the largest ships, passenger or otherwise, owned by British India. They became two of the 'star players' on the still very busy London–East Africa route. Being constructed by an old friend to BI, the Barclay Curle yard at Glasgow, the 540-foot-long *Kenya* had a black hull and white superstructure for the first four years and then changed to the all-white scheme already used on the company's other passenger ships.

The *Kenya* – which could carry 194 passengers in first class and 103 in tourist – had very comfortable, very 1950s, very British, accommodations. First class had six public rooms that extended the length of the promenade deck. The dining room was separate, located a third way from the bow down on C deck. There was a top sports deck and an outdoor pool further aft. First class cabins were grouped on two decks below the public rooms and were either single, double or three-berth. The de luxe staterooms included a sitting area and full bathroom; about a third of the other first class cabins had private facilities. Tourist class public rooms were aft of the superstructure on A deck and their amenities included a separate outdoor pool. Tourist cabins, with two–four berths, had, rather expectedly, the use of public facilities only. The tourist dining room was also on C deck. The *Kenya* and *Uganda* also carried up to six dogs per voyage, housed in a top deck kennel and looked after by the ship's butcher.

C. M. Squarey reviewed countless passenger ships as well as passenger-carrying freighters for his employers, Thomas Cook & Son, in written form from 1949 until 1954. He included these reviews in a book, *The Patient Talks*, published in July 1955. Upon her delivery into service, in September 1951, he wrote of the *Kenya*: 'My knowledge of BI ships is not great; they have all good ships of their kind even if they are not ships over which one is enthused madly. But this *Kenya*, unless I am much mistaken (which I do not believe I am) is positively "pavements ahead", of anything built by the BI Line. She is indeed so very, very good that, while it might be a little excessive to say she can be ranked as a challenge to air transport, nevertheless, I dare to predict that her delightful

Kenya as she was first built. (British India)

Kenya at Cape Town in 1968. (Richard Turnwald Collection)

qualities and quarters will succeed in enticing more than a few people living in East Africa to think twice before taking to the air next time and, instead, say to themselves, "Let's go by the *Kenya* next home leave and really relax, rest and recuperate".'

'The public room space in this ship is very liberal for the numbers carried (175 first class), and their furnishing did command universal and unqualified admiration,' he wrote. 'A distinctive feature about them is the noble height of these rooms. The forward lounge conforms with the wide sweep of the bridge, and the forward end is raised about a foot to produce a balcony effect – a good point. The dome in the centre of the room is beautifully lit, and the circular shaped carpet (a particularly fine specimen) beneath it enhances the appearance of this gracious room. High windows (but quite low enough to see out of when sitting) are a feature not only of this room, but throughout the ship; over the finely carved mantelpiece there is a captivating picture entitled "The Grand Tour".'

Mr Squarey also wrote, as the conclusion of his appraisal, 'The finished and general workmanship on this ship impressed me very much and, furthermore, her delivery date was kept – and she was delivered a completely finished ship. Despite being very light in the water, she ran very smoothly [during an inaugural, invited guests only cruise from Glasgow to London], and even at the stern end vibration was virtually nil. Designed for a service speed of 16 knots, she touched at over 19 knots on trials.'

The *Kenya* relied on cargo as well for her economic balance and so had five cargo holds – two forward, one midships and two aft. Statistically, she had over 375,000 cubic feet of general cargo space and over 22,000 cubic feet of refrigerated. Among her sixteen booms for cargo holding, a seventeenth was for heavy lifting goods. It had a 30-ton lifting capacity.

'Cargo was, of course, very important to the economics of ships like the *Kenya* and *Uganda*', recalled Brian Gregory. 'We tended to carry general cargo outbound and then return from East Africa with frozen meat, coffee, spices, sisal and butter from Kenya. There was also copper, chrome ore, mica, tungsten, asbestos and even arsenic from Rhodesia, cloves from Zanzibar and cotton from Uganda. The general cargo outbound from the UK also included the likes of Morris motor cars, steel from Sheffield and a much welcomed consignment of copies of the latest *Picture Post*. In those times, long before the current age of quick turnaround containerships, we spent fourteen days in London's Royal Albert Docks – five or six days to discharge and then seven to load.'

The building of the *Kenya* and her sister, initially to be called *Karatina*, but then renamed *Uganda*, was first announced in the summer of 1948. The *Kenya*, costing £1.9 million, was the first – being laid down in January 1950 and then launched some ten months later, on 28 November. Beginning with her maiden voyage in August 1951, the steam turbine, twin-screw *Kenya* sailed on an itinerary that would just about remain in place for all her days. After departing from London, where she had a two-week layover for cargo unloading and reloading, she sailed for Gibraltar, sometimes Naples, Port Said, the Suez Canal, Aden, Mombasa, Tanga, Zanzibar, Dar-es-Salaam, Beira and Durban. Homeward, her ports of call were somewhat different – from Durban to Lourenço Marques, Zanzibar, Tanga, Marseilles (where passengers could disembark, get a train to London via

Paris and cut several days off the voyage as well as avoid the notorious Bay of Biscay), Barcelona and Gibraltar.

During her maiden voyage to East Africa, the brand new, flag-bedecked *Kenya* took part in an occasion dubbed 'BI Sunday'. Every berth at Mombasa was occupied by a British India ship, eight in all: *Mantola, Mombasa, Karanja, Modasa, Tabora, Kampala, Sofala* and of course the brand new company flagship *Kenya*.

The *Kenya* and her sister ship had, in fact been built for a very specific trade. According to Hans Andresen, a frequent passenger and longtime resident of East Africa, 'In the late 1940s, Britain had put millions into the Groundnut Scheme in Tanganyika. The port of Mtwara was specially created for the expected large flow of both passengers and freight. Therefore, the *Kenya* as well as the *Uganda* were built as particularly large (for British India) combination passenger-cargo ships for the London–East Africa via Suez trade.'

'Built to carry more passengers in first class and less in tourist class, they catered mostly to European passengers, a few Asians and even fewer Africans', added Andresen. 'They had beautifully finished interiors with very fine woods. Various African artifacts had also been fitted on the ships – such as the tribal drums on the *Kenya* and elephant tusks on the *Uganda*. There were two first class public rooms that I recall especially. It was all leather fittings in the smoking room and soft upholstery in the main lounge. The restaurant was air-conditioned and therefore a popular place. My wife and I liked these ships very much. They were quiet and elegant, and originally had a European band, which was later replaced by an Indian band. The bandleader onboard the *Uganda* was Sonny Souto, who had been recruited from Bombay and was something of a legend within the British India fleet.'

'On the *Kenya* and *Uganda* in the 1950s, you still found the very top end of the colonial trade – the endless ranks of Her Majesty's Service plus top businessmen', recalled Harry Atkinson. 'They certainly still preferred going by sea, enjoying the rest and the care of the voyage. It was also the ideal opportunity for making personal contacts, arranging business deals and sometimes creating life-long friendships. In less expensive tourist class, it was similar in ways, with the lower ranks of the British civil service, settlers, missionaries and budget tourists. To many, those who traveled often, the ships were also like gracious, long-established hotels – passengers enjoyed returning. They knew the officers and staff, were well accustomed to the ways of shipboard life and often shared voyages with friends from prior sailings. It was, in many ways, like a big, floating club. Those voyages had such pleasures – long afternoons in the sun, swimming, tea at four and of course long dinners followed by dancing or maybe a film. And of course, the routing itself was pure romance – passing through the blue waters of the Mediterranean, transiting the Suez Canal, sailing the calm waters of the Red Sea. Then there was the busy, almost exciting commerce of those East African ports.'

'Passengers aboard the *Kenya* and *Uganda* tended to rise early, have breakfast and then were often part of sports committees, for quoits and deck tennis, and afterward enjoyed the pool', added Atkinson. 'After lunch (and there was always a curry on the menu amid more traditional British fare), there continued a tradition to British liners in tropical service: the two to four nap. Then there was tea at four followed by the broadcasting

Strikingly handsome, the brand-new *Kenya* as seen in 1951. (Albert Wilhelmi Collection)

of the BBC World service at five. There was a gong to remind passengers to dress for dinner, mostly in formal attire, followed by a knock on the door by the bathroom steward. You were booked for a specified time and then escorted by the steward to one of the several bathrooms and a tub full of steaming water. Soaking in that tub was, to me, one of the great pleasures of traveling on these BI passenger ships. The dinner menus featured traditional British fare, but often a local item as well. Myself, I well remember the Mulligatawny soup. Tables in the restaurant were very neatly set, all gleaming china and polished silver and white linen, and were looked after by Goan waiters, smartly outfitted and often the son or grandson of an earlier BI waiter or steward.'

'After dinner, there was coffee in the lounge. Then there was dancing – and, using open doors, on deck in warmer climates. It was the popular past time and all done to a Goan band of sometimes questionable skill', concluded Atkinson. 'On some nights, films were shown in the lounge, using a projector positioned in a small booth. Passengers tended to go to bed by eleven, wanting to be up early on the following morning and often lulled to sleep by the hypnotic sounds of the sea through an opened porthole.'

Brian Gregory, later chief engineer of the *Queen Elizabeth 2* and *Queen Mary 2*, served in earlier years aboard the *Uganda*, then still on the East African liner service. 'Ships like the *Uganda* and *Kenya* offered a genteel lifestyle. There weren't any entertainers on board, for example, in those days. The officers and the passengers joined together to create the diversions and amusements. Some 50 per cent of the passengers were British government civil servants and their families, but there were only a few tourists. In later years, as commercial air routes developed, the fathers of these families would fly, but the mothers and children would continue to go by sea. Of course, in the very end, they too had deserted to aircraft.'

'In ports along East Africa, parties were sometimes arranged aboard the *Kenya* and *Uganda*', added Brian Gregory. 'Invited locals would come aboard for drinks, sometimes for dinner and dancing afterward. Many of the local British often enjoyed a traditional Christmas lunch in the air-conditioned comfort of the two-deck high, first class restaurants aboard the *Kenya* and *Uganda*.'

Occasionally, there were special passengers and guests aboard the *Kenya* and *Uganda*. In June 1953, the Sultan of Zanzibar traveled in the *Kenya* from Zanzibar to London and then remained aboard when the flag-dressed ship represented British India on 15 June 1953 at the coronation fleet review at Spithead for Queen Elizabeth II. The *Kenya* was actually on a special three-night coronation review cruise, departing from London and finishing at Plymouth with train connections back to the capital.

Three years later, in 1956, British India celebrated its centenary. Unfortunately, the Suez Crisis of that same year placed something of a cloud over the celebratory tone. The canal, the 'lifeline of the Empire', was closed and ships such as the *Kenya* and *Uganda* had to be rerouted and therefore rescheduled via West Africa on their voyages to and from London. There was a celebratory dinner in London and one at Zanzibar (aboard the *Uganda*), on 13 September, and attended by Sultan and Sultana. Another reception was held at Dar-es-Salaam. Perhaps the most notable event was held on 10 October when Princess Margaret dedicated and opened the new docks at Dar-es-Salaam and then attended a formal banquet aboard the *Kenya*. Traveling aboard the royal yacht *Britannia*, the two ships were berthed together. Delayed by the Suez situation, local dockers rose to the occasion – in preparation for the royal occasion, nearly 4,000 tons of cargo and almost 800 bags of mail were offloaded in two instead of five days. In the intense heat, dockers worked round the clock and actually established a record for an East African port.

'The officers on BI passenger ships, including the *Kenya* and *Uganda*, were often lifetime "career men". They started as cadets and stayed through as officers', added Captain Ian Tompkins. 'Many were devotedly loyal to the company and hugely skilled with the routes, ports and overall operations of the Eastern services. There were captains who knew every sandbar in every port and knew them intimately. The crews of these ships were all Indian – Serangs (bosun's mates), Tindals (mates), Kalassi (seamen), Agwallahs (stokers), Bhandharys (cooks) and of course Goan stewards and waiters. Their duties varied – from polishing brass and painting the decks to serving dinner and laying out evening clothes before dinner.'

There were the occasional incidents aboard these BI passenger ships. 1952 was especially eventful. On 11 May, while inbound in the English Channel, the new *Kenya* had a fire in a cargo hold and had to make an emergency landing at Plymouth; the aged *Modasa* had a fire, one lasting thirteen hours, at Mombasa on 17 November; a day later, off the Seychelles, the *Karanja* rescued passengers and crew from a disabled ship; and on 26 November, the *Uganda* damaged a prop while arriving in Dar-es-Salaam.

The East African service took over a decade before it declined in earnest. Chief Engineer Brian Gregory called it the 'African sunset' of British India. 'Aircraft competition was, in ways, the biggest blow. The airlines just grabbed all the passengers', he said, 'and this included those passengers in third and deck classes. Then, of course, there were the huge political and economic changes. The horrific Mau Mau situation and the failure of the Groundnut Scheme were preludes in the 1950s. South Africa leaving the Commonwealth [in 1960] was another prelude – a prelude to the disappearance of the Union Jack, then the Blue Ensign and finally, of course, BI itself in East Africa. Tanganyika, Kenya, Zanzibar, Nyasaland and Northern Rhodesia became independent within two years [1962–64] and then it all finished with Rhodesia going as well [1965]. Our traditional business, especially among the civil servants but also the settlers, business people and even the tourists, seemed to vanish overnight. It all changed.'

By the early 1970s almost all passenger lines – Union-Castle, Ellerman, Holland-Africa, Messageries Maritimes, Lloyd Triestino and the Portugese Companhia Colonial and Companhia Nacional, were gone. Among other factors, the airlines had largely won out.

While there was some thought at BI's London home office of rebuilding the *Kenya* as either a cruise ship or floating industrial display ship, she was sold, in the end, to Italian breakers at La Spezia. She was dismantled in the summer of 1969.

Above: Another view of the 540-foot-long *Kenya*. (Richard Faber Collection)

Right: The main-line service, the busy run between London and Mombasa, via other European ports, took eighteen days.

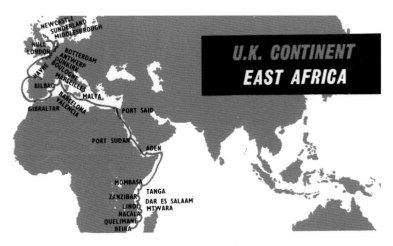

The Service	Two sailings per month in both directions.
The Ships	" KENYA " and " UGANDA " supplemented by fast " C " and " N " class cargo liners.
Accommodation	First Class including de luxe cabins and Tourist Class. " C " class cargo liners have accommodation for 12 passengers , all cabins have private bathrooms.
Freight	General and refrigerated cargo with facilities for the carriage of bulk oil.
Ports of Call	Spanish ports, Marseilles, Port Said, Port Sudan, Aden, Mombasa, Tanga, Zanzibar, Dar es Salaam, Lindi, Mtwara, Nacala, Quelimane, Beira.
Schedule	London to Mombasa in 18 days.

Homeward bound in the English Channel, the *Kenya* was repainted in all-white in 1955. (British India)

15

UGANDA (1952)

Even twin sisters have their differences. Delivered in the summer of 1952, a year after the *Kenya*, the *Uganda*'s most noted difference was her funnel – it was a full 12 feet taller than the flatter one aboard the *Kenya*. To some, the *Kenya* might have looked sleek, but the *Uganda*, with that much taller stack, appeared more regal, more imposing, even more powerful.

Notably, the 14,430-grt ship was British India's 450th vessel since its formation almost a century before, in 1856. And a delightful addition she was too – with an intended service speed of 16 knots, she reached 19.25 knots during her sea trials. She had been launched on 15 January 1952. She set off from London on 2 August on her maiden voyage to East Africa and, as if to add to this inaugural voyage, she passed the homeward bound *Kenya* in the Mediterranean on 9 August. Sadly, however, she was the last BI passenger ship built for the East African run and in fact the very last BI commercial liner.

The passenger quarters on board were very similar to the earlier *Kenya*, but with a slight difference in numbers, with 190 in first class and 109 in tourist class.

While they were smart looking ships, these new BI twins were, in more realistic terms, somewhat dated from the start. They lacked complete air-conditioning, had rather dated decor and perhaps too few cabins with private facilities. The new Lloyd Triestino sisters *Africa* and *Europa*, commissioned just afterward, were far more modern, even sleek looking, had complete air-conditioning (even down in tourist class) and had finer accommodation that included more cabins with at least private shower and toilet facilities. The *Kenya* and *Uganda* had air-conditioning only in the first class restaurant, the hairdressing shop, the hospital and, rather oddly, only the first class staterooms with private bathrooms. In first class, there were eight deluxe, twin-bedded cabins and six deluxe singles with private baths and toilets, and four four-berth rooms with private toilets only.

The 1950s was, in most ways, the last golden age on the Europe–East African passenger run. Business, for passengers as well as cargo, boomed. Everything, it seemed, was plentiful and harbors, railways and road connections were improved.

During her trials, the *Uganda*'s taller funnel is quite evident. It was the distinguishing characteristic between her and the otherwise identical *Kenya*. (British India)

The *Uganda* being berthed at Tilbury in 1956. (British India)

Preparing for another voyage: the *Uganda* is taking on passengers at Tilbury – with P&O's *Chusan* waiting at anchor in the background. (British India)

Independence was still a long way off and so, to many Europeans, East Africa was still, in many ways, a palm tree-fringed paradise. It took seventeen nights to sail from London to Mombasa on, say, the *Kenya* and a two-berth cabin was priced at £130. A round voyage, including long stays for cargo loading and unloading, took sixty-six days. In addition to the BI sisters, rival Union-Castle, also British flag, operated the pre-war built *Durban Castle* and *Warwick Castle* on Round Africa sailings that included numerous ports along the east coast. The all one-class, migrant-style *Bloemfontein Castle* was added in 1950 and then, with some improvements, was followed by the all-cabin class trio of *Rhodesia Castle*, *Braemar Castle* and *Kenya Castle*. These ships were just slightly larger than the *Kenya* and *Uganda*. Then there was a new quartet from Ellerman Lines, the all-first class 107-berth *City of Port Elizabeth*, *City of Exeter*, *City of York* and *City of Durban*. The French, namely Messageries Maritimes, introduced a new quartet in 1952–53 of *Ferdinand des Lesseps*, *Jean Laborde*, *La Bourdonnais* and *Pierri Loti*. Then, serving Portugese East Africa, were four new Portugese liners, the *Imperio*, *Patria*, *Angola* and *Mocambique*. But without question, the *Africa* and *Europa* of Italy's Lloyd Triestino were the greatest competitors, especially to British India, with their fast (nearly 20 knots) speeds and very modern, fully air-conditioned and swimming pool-equipped quarters. While BI held its own, with over a dozen ships including freighters assigned to its East African service, it was a busy, profitable, but also very competitive period. One regular passenger on the East African service added, 'From an English-speaking perspective, Ellerman was considered the best, British India and Holland Africa [which called regularly at Southampton] were second choice and Union-Castle was in third.' BI managers in London studied ideas, in 1961–62, of extensively refitting and modernizing the *Kenya* and *Uganda*, which included installing complete air-conditioning, restyling the public rooms, making them all one class and adding private bathrooms to all cabins. Estimates for such refits surpassed £2 million per ship and eventually these ideas were shelved.

There was another competitor – and one on the rise. In May 1952, even before the *Uganda*, the second new BI East African liner, was commissioned, BOAC's Comet 1 left an otherwise small and compact Heathrow Airport in London for East and South Africa. Kenya could now be reached in sixteen hours rather than seventeen days. While the flight might have seemed extensive (and even exhaustive) – with stops in Rome, Cairo, Khartoum, Entebbe, Livingstone and finally Johannesburg – it ranked as the world's first jet passenger service. In future, air travel would change the face of travel forever. The competition to the likes of British India would start and then gradually accelerate.

As the politics of East Africa changed in the 1960s and the airlines made massive inroads into the passenger business, trading conditions and thus the economics changed for the *Kenya* and *Uganda*. The *Uganda* was the first to go, being pulled off the London–Mombasa–Durban run in January 1967. She found a second life with BI, however, and was converted at Hamburg in 1967–68 to a schools' cruise ship. With her cargo capacity removed, her capacity jumped to 1,200 – 300 adult passengers and 900 school children. The adult passengers used the former first and tourist class quarters; and the youngsters had specially created dormitories.

Looking more yacht-like in all-white, the *Uganda* is seen off Dover. (British India)

Alan Wells, later an entertainer aboard the likes of P&O's *Canberra*, has fond, but also sometimes mournful memories of this last BI school ship and her distinctive role in 'lost era' cruises. Wells was cruise director aboard the *Uganda*. 'There was total segregation between the adults and the children', he recalled. 'The only time the children appeared in the adult section was during their (the children's) fancy dress. They passed through the music room, itself much like a Victorian drawing room. The kids also ran a fun fair in their quarters – having darts, cards and raffles.'

The *Uganda* was another classic passenger-cargo liner of the post-Second World War era. (British India)

Being rebuilt at Hamburg in 1967 as an educational cruise ship. (Steffen Weirauch)

Looking quite different with a rebuilt superstructure, the *Uganda* became a very popular, much beloved cruise ship. (British India)

To many who remember her, *Uganda*'s cruises were reminiscent of possibly grander shipboard days, say, the 1930s. Alan Wells certainly agreed: 'The elevator operator on board was a bearded Indian, straight out of the Raj, and who wore white gloves. On ladies' night, all of the ladies were given a list of all dances and then proceeded to have it filled in.

'There was an entertainments director, which was me, plus a hostess – and that was it. We did everything. At other times, the gaps were filled by officers and staff. The casino night, for example, was worked by the officers.

'Social life onboard often included private cocktail parties since many of the *Uganda* passengers were regulars and therefore previously acquainted with many others. The captain also hosted several parties, using his dayroom, which connected onto a canvas-covered veranda. We also ran a daily tote, hat and flower making sessions, bingo, classical concerts, deck sports and tournaments. Evenings also included frog racing and a ship's concert, both of which were run entirely by the officers. I recall our singing surgeon, the plumber-magician, the chief engineer who did monologues and the engineers who staged a corps d'ballet and it being emceed by the deputy captain. There was also an Indian band, always a quartet, that played before lunch and dinner as well as for after-dinner dancing. It was all just like some grand seaside hotel.'

'The public rooms included a rather splendid ballroom with a Victorian flavor and with windows along each side, looking out onto the sea and aft onto the pool', added Wells. 'The other public room was the smoking room with leather chairs and mounted elephant tusks [sent to P&O's London headquarters after the ship was retired]. Indeed, it was all like a stately gentlemen's club from the nineteenth century. Nothing ever happened here – just chats and drinks. It was a quiet space.

'The theatre was one area where the adults and children merged for specialty and port lectures. The back rows were reserved for the adults. Of course, on board the *Uganda*, all of the shore excursions were included in the passage fares.

'The *Uganda* was almost completely staffed in the hotel areas by Indians. It was service of a lost age. It was all ultra-efficient and cheerful. Chairs were always lifted and pushed, and waiters seemed to catch knives before they fell. Most of the restaurant tables were round and the officers appeared far more often for dinner.

'The food was quite magnificent and also included a desserts trolley, an item now vanished from all P&O and P&O-related liners. Every night and without fail, the headwaiter would inquire about the quality of the meal. Of course, there were lots of curries. There was also far more dressing for dinner, far more black-tie and long gowns.

'The *Uganda* lured a special type of passenger – mostly retirees and mostly professional people. Consequently, the age range was rather high. We had passengers well in their eighties, some in their nineties. There were virtually never any children traveling in the adult quarters. We had lots of retired military, ex-Army and the old colonial set – lord this and lady that. Since many of the passengers were regulars and therefore knew one another, they were the easiest group to get dancing. They were always a great audience and wonderfully good hearted. They always helped decorate the lounge before a party or special occasion. They were also a very well-traveled group, the type of people who like lots of non-fiction in the library.

End of the day: the *Uganda* departs after another port call. (Luis Miguel Correia)

BI
Discovery Cruises
1982.

BI Discovery Cruises, 1982. (Author's Collection)

BI Educational
Cruises
1982

21st anniversary

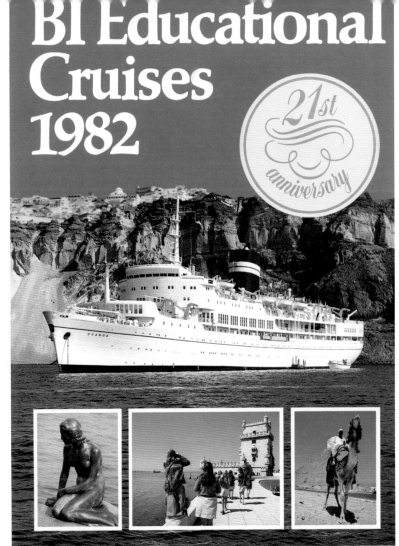

BI Educational Cruises, 1982. (Author's Collection)

The ss 'UGANDA'
Society

Formed to ensure the prese
vation of this much loved ves
and the continued use of h
facilities for the benefit of a
as a student interest centre, a
activity centre and a maritin
exhibition centre

We invite you to contact
for details and to join th
worthwhile and excitin
project.

72 Downs Road,
Coulsdon,
Surrey CR3 1AF

Tel. Downland 54773

A commemorative leaflet from the *Uganda* Society to preserve the ship in 1984–85. (Uganda Society)

Sailing from Lisbon: the *Uganda* gets underway. (Luis Miguel Correia)

'The children slept in dormitories, in the aft section of the ship, that I rather vaguely recall as being two-tier with twenty or so to a dorm', concluded Alan Wells. 'They were usually in the thirteen to sixteen age range. During the days at sea, they attended classes and lectures. At night, discos seemed to be quite popular. They were chaperoned by teachers, of course. These busy souls, like lecturers, slept in the adult quarters mostly.'

According to Captain Tompkins, who was master of the ship, 'The adult passengers on these *Uganda* cruises were good, caring, very traditional English people. They traveled for travel's sake. These passengers loved school ship cruising and life on board was very special. Of course, they enjoyed the lecturers and headmasters, and the wonderful ports of call and excursions, which were included. They enjoyed the all-Indian staff and this included the three-piece Goan band. The kids entertained themselves, setting-up discos, shows, fancy dress, etc. Adults could come down and watch.'

'We also did National Trust cruises, usually one a year, to places like St Kilda, a bird sanctuary, and one foreign port like Bergen or Copenhagen. We carried bird lecturers on these trips. On these trips, the adults lived in the dorms', added Captain Tompkins. 'There was also an annual Catholic Church Pilgrimage, a cruise from Dublin to Italy or Portugal and mostly with adults.'

Life for the thirty-year-old *Uganda* was disrupted and all but changed forever by the early 1980s. On 2 April 1982 Argentina invaded and captured the Falkland Islands. A day later Britain pledged liberation and that a huge task force would be sent to the South Atlantic. Among others, the big 2,200-berth *Canberra* of P&O Cruises was called up in the first week. Momentum grew and included rumors that the royal yacht *Britannia* would be sent south as well, in the role of hospital ship. Instead, on 10 April, while at Alexandria on a Mediterranean cruise (with 315 cabin passengers and 940 children aboard), the *Uganda* was requisitioned for hospital duties, ordered to Naples to offload all passengers and then proceed to Gibraltar for conversion. In a matter of days, with vivid red crosses painted along her sides and on her funnel, she was off to southern waters carrying 135 medical staff including 12 doctors and 40 nurses. She gave heroic service and, after 113 days, was given a rousing welcome when she finally returned to the UK, to Southampton, on 9 August.

P&O Captain Bob Ellingham was sent to Gibraltar in April 1982 to help supervise the conversion of the *Uganda*. He recalled, 'After her duty during the Falklands War, the *Uganda* went on a two-year charter to the British government as a relay ship for both forces and ships' personnel between Ascension and the Falklands. P&O received a very good income, estimated at $85 million for the two years, on their thirty-three-year-old ship. The *Uganda* was still very sound and could probably have gone on forever but, of course, she needed more and more repairs. She just managed 13 knots at top speed and that was it.'

Refitted and restored for educational cruising by mid-September, the stint in the Falklands caused a disruption and there was a slump in passenger as well as school bookings. The 1983 season was looking light, in fact very light, to the sometimes ruthless P&O accountants in London. 'Even before the call-up for duty in the Falklands, the *Uganda*'s fate was already sealed. The old school cruise trade was disappearing', added Captain Tompkins. 'School budgets were tighter and fares climbed to

Anchored in the Thames: the *Uganda* at London. (Alex Duncan)

Off to war during the Falklands Campaign in 1982. (P&O)

Another view of the *Uganda* in military dress in 1982.
(Steffen Weirauch)

Return from duty: the *Uganda* returns to Southampton in August 1982
– with the gray-hulled *Queen Elizabeth 2* in the background. (P&O)

Grand welcome: crowds at Southampton welcome the *Uganda* home from duties in the South Atlantic. (P&O)

Return to service: the *Uganda* resumed cruising in September 1982. Another heroic veteran of South Atlantic service, the *Canberra*, is berthed to the left. (P&O)

£300 per student. It had become too much – it was no longer so easily affordable.'

When the British government decided it still needed a troopship for relay sailings between Ascension and Port Stanley, the *Uganda* was chartered to the Ministry of Defence for over two years, beginning in January 1983 and until April 1985. She was very hard worked after those two years, having been at sea for nearly 500 days. On the outside, she was covered in great streaks of rust. She returned to the UK, was handed back to P&O at Falmouth on 27 April and days later moved to the River Fal in Cornwall for lay-up.

Captain Tompkins saw the laid-up *Uganda* in the River Fal: 'She was full of rust and decay and was listing. Goodies like the elephant tusks in the lounge were already gone, but the wood veneers were still there. In the Verandah Cafe, the carpet was pulled back, revealing the old maple dance floor. The *Uganda* was dark and empty and smelling badly. Only the scrappers were interested. The specially organized Uganda Society wanted to save her, but it all came to nothing.'

Her future had little hope. In the spring of 1986, after a year at anchor, she was sold to Taiwanese shipbreakers, being delivered to the London-based Triton Ship Delivery Company and renamed *Triton* for the long, slow voyage out to Kaohsiung.

On 20 May the late Keith Byass, a noted British marine photographer and artist, witnessed the final departure (from her moorings on the Fal) of the final British India liner. 'It was a very moving experience – with bags of tears, car horns blowing, etc. The rust on her hull was a sorry sight and, as she got underway, her smoke nearly blotted out the entire scene.' She was routed via Suez, a nostalgic last passage to her old days on the East African run. It was a troubled trip, however – the start was delayed by boiler problems, she was plundered by thieves at Port Said and then refused entry for bunkers at Jeddah. In all, the trip took almost two months, but a dramatic ending was ahead.

A month or so after arriving at Kaohsiung (on 15 July), when the rust-covered ex-*Uganda* was already grounded in preparation for scrapping, she was lashed by tropical storm Wayne (with winds over 40 knots) and capsized. On her side, a complete loss, the *Uganda*'s once dominant and immaculate funnel was the last to bear the black and white colors of British India. The remains of the ship were gradually demolished beginning in 1992.

Outward bound: the *Uganda* passes the *Sea Princess* at Southampton, September 1982. (P&O)

End of her days: the *Uganda* laid up in the River Fal in Cornwall in 1985. (Author's Collection)

Last voyage: tugs shift the *Uganda* in May 1986 at the beginning of her final voyage out to the Far East and the scrappers. (Author's Collection)

The late J. K. Byass's painting of the final departure. (Author's Collection)

Farewell *Uganda*! (Uganda Society)

16

NEVASA (1956)

British India's centenary year was 1956 and it seemed almost fitting that the company added its largest passenger ship ever that same year in July. She was also the last BI passenger ship to be built. Constructed by Barclay Curle at Glasgow, she was also one of the last British passenger ships to be constructed solely for peacetime trooping. She also represented improved standards – she was the first British trooper to have stabilizers and, for added comfort, some of her quarters were air-conditioned.

Ordered in the summer of 1954 and launched in November 1955 as the *Nevasa*, this 20,500 tonner entered service with a seemingly solid future: a fifteen-year charter to the British government. A near-sister, the *Oxfordshire*, was completed a year later, but for the Bibby Line. She too was given an extended charter. Accommodations on board the twin-screw *Nevasa* were arranged as 220 first class, 110 second class, 69 third class and 931 troops. First class had one- to three-berth cabins, second class two- to four-berth, third class three- to four-berth and all while the troops used standee bunks.

Plans changed, however, and by 1962 the British government abruptly ended peacetime trooping by sea. The 609-foot-long *Nevasa* was suddenly out of work and soon sent to lay up in the River Fal in Cornwall. Alternately, the *Oxfordshire* was actually sold off, being thoroughly rebuilt as an all-tourist class passenger liner for the Europe–Australia service and low-fare around the world trade. She entered service as the 1,910-passenger *Fairstair* sailing for the very popular Italian-based Sitmar Line.

Prompted by the success of the earlier, older, smaller ships, it took three years before the *Nevasa* was recommissioned by British India as an educational cruise ship. She was refitted in the fall of 1964.

'The *Nevasa* and *Uganda* were very interesting ships, unique in the British passenger ship fleet', said Robert Bell, who worked in the beauty salon aboard both ships. 'They were two class: 1,000 kids in separate, dormitory-style quarters and about 300 adult passengers, who used upper-deck staterooms and who had separate public rooms. My work was almost entirely involved with the adults. We sailed from various British ports: London,

The largest British India passenger ship was the 20,500-grt *Nevasa* seen here at Southampton. (Roger Sherlock)

Restyled for educational cruising in 1964. (Michael D. J. Lennon)

The *Nevasa* anchored at Valletta on Malta. (Luis Miguel Correia Collection)

Another cruise begins! Embarking passengers at the Tilbury Landing Stage, London. (Alex Duncan)

Liverpool and Glasgow as well as Cardiff, Newcastle, Greenock and Invergordon. Equally the voyages themselves were diverse, on voyages from seven to fourteen days. In summer, we'd cruise to the north: to the Baltic, the Norwegian fjords and port cities in Northern Europe such as Hamburg, Amsterdam and Antwerp. But mostly, we would head for the sun: to Spain and Portugal, the Mediterranean and West Africa including the Canary Islands and Madeira. In later years, we would sometimes base the ships in the Mediterranean and fly out the passengers and the students to the likes of Malta, Venice, Athens [Piraeus] and Istanbul.'

Menu

B R E A K F A S T

Juices: Tomato   Orange   Pineapple

Fresh Grapefruit

Cornflakes   All Bran   Sugar Puffs

Rice Crispies   Weetabix

Rolled Oatmeal

Smoked Haddock

Grilled Bacon   Pork Sausages

Eggs: Fried   Poached   Boiled

Scrambled   Turned

Omelette: Plain   Asparagus

Cold Ham   and   Tongue

White & Brown Rolls   Toast   Cream Scones

Sultana Brioche

Marmalade   Strawberry Jam   Honey

Tea   Coffee   Cocoa

* * * * *

First Thing

In bed
early morning tea and
the ship's newspaper—
the day's events

Mornings at sea
are indescribably
beautiful

Educational cruising: life aboard the *Uganda* and *Nevasa*! (British India)

How busy leisure is

At your immediate disposal, activity or relaxation.

Relaxing days at sea! (British India)

'During the sea days, there were wonderful lectures in a large cinema-auditorium', added Bell. 'The adults could attend (in separate seating) and the speakers were superb teachers, professors, historians, geographers, archeologists and even explorers. The talks were mostly about the history and geography of our destinations. Altogether, it opened a "greater window" for the youngsters. They also did readings in the ships' large libraries, made projects and performed in presentations on stage. In the evenings, there were social events, parties, talent shows, skits and an always popular disco. The officers of the ship along with the teacher-chaperones attended these and always enforced a "lights out" curfew. Each dormitory had its own head, a monitor of sorts. In the early 1970s, a two-week cruise for a student might cost $200, an amount that could be raised by the students themselves doing a newspaper route or some after-school job. Of course, parents and relatives often helped with the fares and sometimes the schools themselves assisted. These cruises were not considered so much a holiday, but an enriching, once-in-a-lifetime educational experience. In later years, by the early 1980s, it all became too expensive, however, and the BI student trade fell away.

'Onboard, everything usually went well. An exception was the fear of terrorism in the Eastern Mediterranean, often in places such as Greece, Turkey and Yugoslavia. We always had to check for mines after visiting Egypt and Israel.'

Actually, Robert Bell worked mostly with the adult passengers, usually an older breed of travelers that preferred myths and ruins over the cha-cha classes and jackpot bingo games associated with ordinary cruise ships. 'We had lots of steady passengers, all of them English and often retired', he remembered. 'Many were old British military types and, among them, many remembered the days of the old Imperial Raj. The decor of a ship such as *Uganda* suited them with wood-paneled lounges, leather chairs and a smoking room for after-dinner coffee and brandies. They were very loyal passengers, who had already been on six or more BI school voyages. There was great regularity. They tended to know one another from prior trips. Of course, there were many "characters" among them – old colonels wearing monocles and going ashore with walking sticks and straw hats, and who in the evening wore war medals on aged dinner jackets. They knew the crew and the crew knew them. There was a sort of club-like familiarity, a shipboard world where time had all but stopped.'

This school cruise trade began to fall away when marine fuel oil prices greatly escalated – from as much as $35 to $95 a ton – in the mid-1970s. Almost abruptly and certainly prematurely, the nineteen-year-old *Nevasa* went to scrap in 1975 out on Taiwan. The *Uganda* carried on alone for a few more years.

'The *Nevasa* went far too soon, but it was the dawning of a new age in ship economics', added Captain Tompkins. 'Steamships like her became much too expensive to operate. There was no room for even the slightest profit.'

The end for schools cruising for Robert Bell came with the very final cruise of the *Nevasa* in January 1975. Her next voyage was from Malta, bound for those Far Eastern scrappers. 'We flew a long paying-off pennant on that last cruise to the Mediterranean. Then we sailed to Valletta on Malta. It was an eerie voyage. There were no passengers and so there was no noise. The lounges and corridors were empty. There had been cutbacks and so there was even less crew. When we finally reached Malta, we tied up next to a supertanker. When we

Siesta

A time for sunshine companionship and reading

The easy life! (British India)

Shades of evening

Social pleasures are exhilarating in the right atmosphere.

After-dinner activities! (British India)

Your Cabin

s.s. "UGANDA" Outside three berth Cabin (Grade 'E')

s.s. "UGANDA" Two-bedded Cabin with facilities (Grade 'A')

s.s. "UGANDA" Single Cabin (Grade 'B')

s.s. "UGANDA" Special Cabin.

A large proportion of "UGANDA's" cabins have private facilities and those without windows or portholes are air-conditioned.

Cabin accommodation aboard the *Uganda*. (British India)

s.s. "NEVASA" Single berth Cabin (Grade 'B')

Your home at sea

s.s. "NEVASA" Three berth Cabin (Grade 'E')

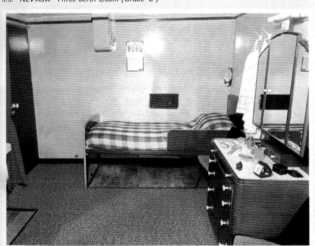

All "NEVASA's" cabins have windows or portholes.

Quarters in the *Nevasa*.

Domed funnel: The *Nevasa* was an attractive-looking passenger ship. (British India)

eventually left the *Nevasa*, in the early morning darkness, we had to walk across the tanker. Then we had to walk down 200 feet on a very narrow ladder and all while carrying our bags. To me, it was petrifying. There was no full gangway and so it was one step at a time. It was a strange ending to a sad day.'

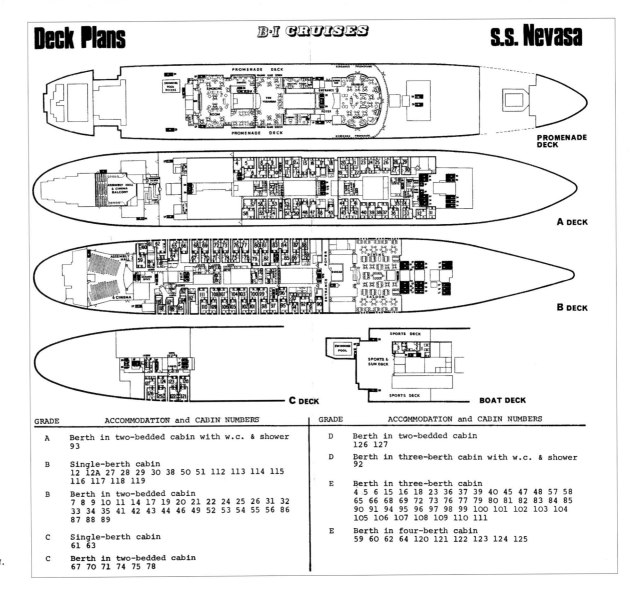

PROMENADE DECK

A DECK

B DECK

C DECK   BOAT DECK

GRADE	ACCOMMODATION and CABIN NUMBERS
A	Berth in two-bedded cabin with w.c. & shower 93
B	Single-berth cabin 12 12A 27 28 29 30 38 50 51 112 113 114 115 116 117 118 119
B	Berth in two-bedded cabin 7 8 9 10 11 14 17 19 20 21 22 24 25 26 31 32 33 34 35 41 42 43 44 46 49 52 53 54 55 56 86 87 88 89
C	Single-berth cabin 61 63
C	**Berth in two-bedded cabin** 67 70 71 74 75 78

GRADE	ACCOMMODATION and CABIN NUMBERS
D	Berth in two-bedded cabin 126 127
D	Berth in three-berth cabin with w.c. & shower 92
E	Berth in three-berth cabin 4 5 6 15 16 23 36 37 39 40 45 47 48 57 58 65 66 68 69 72 73 76 77 79 80 81 82 83 84 85 90 91 94 95 96 97 98 99 100 101 102 103 104 105 106 107 108 109 110 111
E	Berth in four-berth cabin 59 60 62 64 120 121 122 123 124 125

Passenger deck plan of the *Nevasa*.
(Andrew Kilk Collection)

Robert Bell returned to England by air and so ended his affiliation with British India and an interesting phase of British sea travel: school cruising.

The nineteen-year-old *Nevasa*, also a victim of soaring fuel oil prices for steam-powered passenger ships, was sold to Taiwanese scrappers, the Nan Feng Steel Enterprises Company, and scrapped in the summer of 1975 at Kaohsiung.

It had all long passed! By 2015 it will be a quarter of a century since the last links to British India were about – the wreckage out on Taiwan of the ex-*Uganda* and the *Nancowry*, the former finishing her days for the Shipping Corporation of India. The company's long, colorful history is worthy of an extensive study, but in this work, I felt another nostalgic look of its post-Second World War passenger fleet was worthy of a reminder. Although I missed seeing these ships, I can visualize, say, the *Kenya* loading in the London Docks, the *Kampala* at Durban preparing for another voyage to the Seychelles and India, the *Dumra* discharging at Bombay after another circuit around the Persian Gulf, the *Sangola* anchored in Hong Kong harbor surrounded by barges, floating cranes and junks and small armies of happy, excited school children coming ashore from the *Uganda*. What a fascinating fleet!

Here's to BI and its charismatic passenger ships!

Meeting at sea: *Nevasa* passes HMS *Bulwark*. (British India)

Summer cruise: the *Nevasa* moored in Norway's beautiful Geirangerfjord. (British India)

Another sailing: the *Nevasa* at Southampton. (Luis Miguel Correia)

Final sailing: minus some of her lifeboats, the *Nevasa* departs from Valletta on her final voyage to Far Eastern scrappers. (Michael Cassar)

BIBLIOGRAPHY

Crowdy, Michael and Kevin O'Donoghue (eds), *Marine News* (Kendal: World Ship Society, 1964–2014).

Devol, George and Thomas Cassidy (eds), *Ocean & Cruise News* (Stamford: World Ocean & Cruise Society, 1980–2014).

Dunn, Laurence, *Passenger Liners* (Southampton: Adlard Coles Ltd, 1961).

Dunn, Laurence, *Passenger Liners* (revised edition) (Southampton: Adlard Coles Ltd, 1965).

Haws, Duncan. *Merchant Ships: British India Steam Navigation Company* (Burwash: TCL Publications, 1987).

Kohler, Peter, *Sea Safari: British India S. N. Co. African Ships & Services* (Abergavenny: P. M. Heaton Publishing, 1995).

Miller, William H., *British Ocean Liners: A Twilight Era 1960–85* (New York: W. W. Norton & Co., 1986).

Miller, William H., *Pictorial Encyclopedia of Ocean Liners, 1864–1994* (Mineola: Dover Publications Inc., 1995).

Miller, William H., *Picture History of British Ocean Liners* (Mineola: Dover Publications Inc., 2001).

Plowman, Peter, *Australian Cruise Ships* (Sydney: Rosenberg Publishing Pty Ltd, 2007).

Squarey, C. M., *The Patient Talks* (London: Thomas Cook & Company Ltd, 1955).

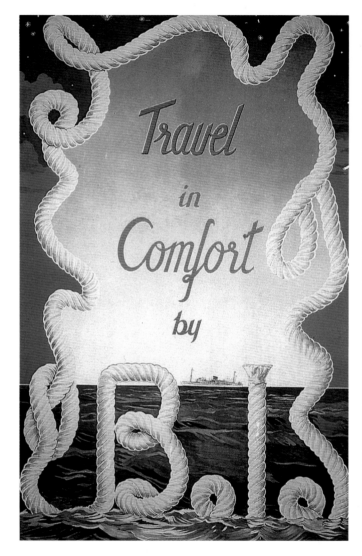

British India advertising material.